WORLD BANK WORKING PAPER NO. 77

Participatory Approaches to Attacking Extreme Poverty

Case Studies Led by the International Movement ATD Fourth World

Edited by Xavier Godinot and Quentin Wodon

THE WORLD BANK
Washington, D.C.

ISBN-10: 0-8213-6625-4   ISBN-13: 978-0-8213-6625-7
eISBN: 0-8213-6626-2
ISSN: 1726-5878   DOI: 10.1596/978-0-8213-6625-7

Xavier Godinot is the Director of the Research and Training Institute of the International Movement ATD Fourth World. Quentin Wodon is Lead Poverty Specialist in the Poverty Reduction and Economic Management Unit of the Africa Region Department of the World Bank.

Library of Congress Cataloging-in-Publication Data has been requested.

Contents

Foreword vii

Abstract ix

Acknowledgments xi

1. Participatory Approaches to Attacking Extreme Poverty: An Overview 1
    Charles Courtney, Xavier Godinot, and Quentin Wodon
    Overview of the Contributions in This Volume 3
    Seminar at the World Bank to Discuss the Issue of Extreme Poverty 6
    Conclusion: Where Do We Go from Here? 8

PART I: Three Types of Knowledge on Poverty

2. A Knowledge That Leads to Action 13
    Joseph Wresinski
    Academic Knowledge and Mobilization for Action 14
    Without Freedom of Thought, No Communication 15
    The Secret Garden of the Poorest of the Poor 17
    Restoring Thinking, Supporting the Effort of the Fourth World to Know 19
    An Action That Thinks and Communicates Itself 20
    A Committee Ready for Action 21

3. Making Services Work for Very Poor People: Comments
    on the World Development Report 2004 23
    Xavier Godinot
    The Nature of Chronic Poverty and the Challenge of Its Eradication 25
    The Uncertainty of Statistics on Extreme Poverty 28
    The Knowledge Building Process of the WDR Report 30
    The Shortage of Truly Participatory Research on Poverty 33
    Conclusion 34

PART II: Experiences from Developing Countries

4. Making Health Services Work for Poor People: Ten Years
    of Work in Tananarive, Madagascar 37
    Chantal Laureau, Caroline Blanchard, and Xavier Godinot
    Living Conditions and Health Care Provision in Tananarive 37
    The Decision to Carry Out an Early Childhood Program (1989–1990) 40

Starting Point: Lack of Understanding and a Divide Between
the Hospitals and the Inhabitants 41

Implementation of the Knowledge-Health Program Around
Those in Early Childhood.. 42

Extending the Knowledge-Health Program 44

The Development Books... 44

Dialog with Health Professionals and Medical Bodies.............. 45

Writing a Book on the Health of Very Young Children 46

People and a Neighborhood Gaining Freedom and Pride.......... 47

Some Lessons Learned from the Program............................... 49

5. **Taking the Time to Learn from the Poor in Tanzania** 55
Niek Tweehuysen and Andrew Hayes

Encountering the Very Poor 56

Enabling the Very Poor to Join Forces 60

International Day for the Eradication of Poverty....................... 61

Other Sources of Knowledge 63

Partners in Development 66

Conclusion... 71

6. **Enabling Children to Learn in Latin America.** 73
International Movement ATD Fourth World (Bolivia, Guatemala, and Peru Teams)

Reaching the Poorest Children Through Street Libraries in Peru.............. 73

Understanding the Life of Poor Children and their Parents:
Doña Elena's Family in Guatemala... 79

Enabling Children to Learn from Each Other: The Tapori
Network in Bolivia.. 83

Conclusion... 88

PART III: Experiences from Developed Countries

7. **The Story of the "Unleashing Hidden Potential" Seminar
in the United States.** 91
Carl Egner

Roots of the project.. 93

The Street Library in East New York 94

A New Project in Boston... 96

Preparing the Seminar.. 97

The Unleashing Hidden Potential Seminar............................... 99

After the Seminar... 104

Conclusion... 105

8. Another Approach to Poverty Indicators in Belgium 107
Johan Bellens, Régis De Muylder, Béatrice Meurant,
Henk Van Hootegem, and Frank Vereecken

Goals of the Research-Action-Training and Method 109

Results. 109

General Reflections 114

Conclusions 115

LIST OF BOXES

1.1 A Delegation of Families in Poverty is Received at the World Bank 7

4.1 Infant and Child Mortality in Madagascar 40

4.2 Dialog Between the Very Poor and Health Services 45

4.3 A Nurse's Experience 46

4.4 Leaving Fear Behind: The Account in 2004 of the Path
Traveled by One Mother 48

4.5 A Mother's Account, End of 2004 48

5.1 Paul 59

5.2 Andrew 63

5.3 Saidi 65

5.4 Hamis 70

6.1 One Day in a Street Library in El Bosque 76

6.2 Gerson. 81

6.3 Tapori Activities in Lourdes' and Gema's Schools 85

6.4 Juanita (By a Member of the ATD Fourth World Bolivian Team) 87

Foreword

Today, governments and international organizations are scaling up programs for the reduction of poverty, but they have difficulties in reaching the poorest. The extreme poor suffer from many handicaps (lack of financial resources, education, employment, housing, health care, empowerment), which have a mutually reinforcing impact, and often lead to social exclusion. Together, the isolation and the state of deprivation in which the very poor live imply that traditional development programs and policies which may be effective in helping the poor may not always work for the poorest.

Reaching the poorest in society remains a challenge for NGOs, governments and aid agencies that design and implement poverty reduction programs. To understand why as well as identify practical ways of moving forward, a seminar on extreme poverty was organized at the World Bank in October 2005. The case studies compiled in this book emerged from that seminar and they show how helping the very poor to emerge from poverty requires not only extra public resources, effort, and time, but also a broader approach to development policy. In particular it is important to learn from the poor themselves as to how they cope with multiple deprivations and what is needed from their point of view to attack extreme poverty. For example, many factors prevent the very poor from using services that would make a difference in their life. This includes lack of physical access as well as lack of affordability. Beyond those issues, cultural and behavioral issues—including a lack of trust between the very poor and broader society—also reduce the take-up of social services by the extreme poor.

The lessons learned from the case studies presented in this book have implications for grassroots organizations working with the poor, for local and national governments, and even for international financial organizations. Working with the extreme poor requires a long-term process, not one-shot interventions. Efforts are needed to strengthen the capacity of the extreme poor for transforming their own lives, and to build a consensus for a new social contract in which the extreme poor (and excluded people in general) assume the role of subjects in the process of transforming the institutions that regulate decisionmaking as well as the distribution and redistribution of assets. This requires among others a new type of relationship between external agents (such as government officials, civil society volunteers and community organizers) and the very poor. There is also a need to generate better action-oriented knowledge to help the extreme poor in understanding and transforming the reality in which they live. In short, the design of projects aimed at reaching the very poor should begin by asking a very simple question: Will this project allow the poorest the opportunity to advance towards greater autonomy and freedom rather than remaining in a cycle of deprivation and dependency?

Sudhir Shetty
Sector Director, Poverty Reduction and Economic Management
Africa Region, World Bank

Abstract

Relying on contributions from the International Movement ATD Fourth World, this book deals with questions such as: What does it mean to live in poverty, and especially in extreme poverty? How can the very poor be reached through development projects? How can we assess whether projects succeed in changing the life of the poorest? In answering these questions, the emphasis is on exploring what type of knowledge is needed to fight extreme poverty. A key argument is that apart from academic knowledge, a concerted effort is needed to listen to the knowledge of the poor themselves, as well as to the knowledge of practitioners who are engaged with the poor on a daily basis to fight poverty. After the introductory chapter, the text of a speech by Joseph Wresinski (founder of the International Movement ATD Fourth World) at a congress of social scientists held at UNESCO, is reproduced. The next contribution is based on comments by the International Movement ATD Fourth World on the World Bank's *World Development Report 2004 Making Services Work for Poor People*. Thereafter, case studies are provided on participatory approaches to attacking extreme poverty in both developing countries (Madagascar and Tanzania, as well as Bolivia, Guatemala and Peru) and developed countries (the United States and Belgium).

Acknowledgments

This report is a product of the Front Office of the Poverty Reduction and Economic Management Sector Unit in the Sub-Saharan Africa Vice-Presidency at the World Bank, in collaboration with the International Movement ATD Fourth World. The report provides contributions from the International Movement ATD Fourth World on "Participatory Approaches to Attacking Poverty," together with an introduction. Several contributions prepared for this report were presented at a seminar on extreme poverty that was held at the World Bank on October 19, 2005. The preparation of the report benefited from a grant from the Belgian Poverty Reduction Partnership Program, a trust fund from the Belgian Development Cooperation Agency managed at the World Bank. The report benefited from comments by Estanislao Gacitua-Mario who served as peer reviewer.

Chapter 2 reproduces the text of a speech by Joseph Wresinski (founder of the International Movement ATD Fourth World) at a congress of social scientists held at UNESCO. The chapter was published in French in 1991 in *Revue Quart Monde* (No. 140) under the title "La Pensée des plus pauvres dans une connaissance qui conduise au combat." The chapter was translated in English by Alice Husson, Bruno Tardieu, Xavier Louveaux, and Charles Sleeth and revised in 2005 by Charles Courtney.

Chapter 3 was prepared in 2003 by the Research and Training Institute of the International Movement ATD Fourth World and written by Xavier Godinot, with comments by Jean-Marie Anglade, Jason French, Jean-Pierre Gollé, Xavier Louveaux, Diana Skelton, Thierry Viard, Susie Devins, and Eugen Brand. Elements of this contribution were discussed and presented by Xavier Godinot on the occasion of two visits to Washington, D.C. (in October 2002 and October 2003) as an invited speaker to the World Bank's Poverty Day, a training event for World Bank staff.

Chapter 4 was written by Caroline Blanchard, drawing heavily on several unpublished papers written by Chantal Laureau, who spent ten years in Madagascar working as a physician in a very poor neighborhood of Antananarivo. It was revised and completed by Xavier Godinot and Chantal Laureau. In April 2003, elements of this contribution were presented by Chantal Laureau and Sophie Razanakoto to Shantayanan Devarajan, Director of the *World Development Report 2004 Making Services Work for Poor People*, and Agnes Soucat, Senior Health Economist at the World Bank, during a meeting at the office of ATD Quart Monde France in Paris.

Chapter 5 is an edited version of a paper first published in 2003 by the International Movement ATD Fourth World as a self-standing working document entitled "Three Years of Learning in Tanzania." The document was written by the Tanzania team of the International Movement ATD Fourth World under the overall coordination of Niek Tweehuysen and Andrew Hayes, and edited for this report by Rahel Kassahun and Quentin Wodon.

Chapter 6 was originally written in Spanish in 2002 by Jean-Marie Anglade together with the Guatemala, Peru, and Bolivia teams of the International Movement ATD Fourth World. These teams comprise of José Dimas Pérez Vanegas (Guatemala), María Antonieta Pino de Navarrate, Yaque Gusmán Oviedo, Karely Paredes Ochoa, Marco Aurelio Ugarte Ochoa, Nicolás Vladimiro Pino Amache, and Charles Sleeth (all from the Peru team), and María Julia Pino Amache and Charo Carasco Cuba (Bolivia team). The chapter was translated and edited for this report by Diego Angel-Urdinola and Quentin Wodon.

Chapter 7 was written by Carl Egner who used various materials dealing with the Unleashing Hidden Potential seminar that was organized by Fourth World Movement/USA in New York in 2000. In particular, the chapter builds on a CD-Rom and four issues of the *Fourth World Journal* published by the Fourth World Movement in the United States from September 2001 to November 2003.

Chapter 8 was written by Johan Bellens, Régis De Muylder, Béatrice Meurant, Henk Van Hootegem, and Frank Vereecken, who made up the pedagogical team that led the research-action-training program "Another approach to poverty indicators in Belgium." This was a two-year program that gathered 23 participants, including 12 who live in poverty chosen from Belgian NGOs that give the poor a chance to express their opinions. The other participants were academics, representatives of various government bodies and institutions, and the pedagogical team.

The views expressed in the various chapters of this report are those of the authors, and they do not necessarily represent those of the World Bank, its Executive Directors, or the countries they represent, nor do they necessarily represent the views of the Belgian donor agency which helped fund this work.

CHAPTER 1

Participatory Approaches to Attacking Extreme Poverty: An Overview

Charles Courtney, Xavier Godinot, and Quentin Wodon[1]

Relying on contributions from the International Movement ATD Fourth World, this report deals with questions such as: What does it mean to live in poverty, and especially in extreme poverty? How can the very poor be reached through development projects? How can we assess whether projects succeed in changing the life of the poorest? In answering these questions, the emphasis is on exploring what type of knowledge is needed to fight extreme poverty. A key argument is that apart from academic knowledge, a concerted effort is needed to listen to the knowledge of the poor themselves, as well as to the knowledge of practitioners who are engaged with the poor on a daily basis to fight poverty.

There is a fine line between being poor and living in extreme poverty. The poorest are in such a state of deprivation that policies which may be effective for the poor may not work for them. Extreme poverty affects all aspects of life and, consequently, comprehensive policies are needed to fight it, which may well require extra public resources and time. At the grassroots level, standing by the poorest in the long-term also requires a special commitment and confidence in their ability to build a better life for themselves.

---

1. Charles Courtney is the president of the Fourth World Movement in the USA and a retired philosophy professor from Drew University. Xavier Godinot is the director of the Research and Training Institute of the International Movement ATD Fourth World. Quentin Wodon is a Lead Poverty Specialist for Africa at the World Bank. The views expressed in this chapter are those of the authors, and they do not necessarily represent those of the World Bank, its Executive Directors, or the countries they represent.

Recent international conferences and summits have included the issue of extreme poverty in their agenda.[2] In September 2000, the United Nations Millennium Declaration adopted by 147 heads of State asserted[3]:

> We will spare no effort to free our fellow men, women and children from the abject and dehumanizing conditions of extreme poverty, to which more than a billion of them are currently subjected. We are committed to making the right to development a reality for everyone and to freeing the entire human race from want.

Yet the same declaration reads "we resolve further to halve, by the year 2015, the proportion of the world's people whose income is less than one dollar a day and the proportion of people who suffer from hunger etc." What about the other half? While the target of halving poverty by 2015 was dictated by realism (and we now know that the target is not likely to be achieved in many countries, especially in Sub-Saharan Africa), it may well be that the Millennium Development Goals run the risk that priority be given to the less poor among the poor at the expense of the others, in order to meet the targets.

Also, while over time a larger number of reports and studies have been dealing with the issue of extreme poverty, it is not actually clear whether national societies and the international community have taken the true measure of what is needed to fight extreme poverty and to join the very poor in their daily struggles.

The focus of the present report is on reaching a better understanding of extreme poverty by recognizing the various types of knowledge that are required in order to inform the fight against extreme poverty. A key argument of the report is that apart from academic knowledge, we need to listen to the knowledge of the poor themselves, as well as to the knowledge of those who are engaged with them on a daily basis to fight poverty. Today, while all three types of knowledge are somewhat recognized, academic knowledge is still given prominence, sometimes to the detriment of the other two types of knowledge, with potentially important implications for policy.

Economic definitions of the extreme poor in developing countries often refer to households whose income or consumption per capita is less than a given threshold, such as one dollar a day. While such definitions have the merit of providing a standard by which to measure progress, the very poor do not use such definitions to communicate what extreme poverty means to them. According to the experience of the International Movement ATD Fourth World, extreme poverty results not only from insufficient financial resources, but from a lack of basic securities in many different areas, for example: education, employment, housing, health care, and participation in civil society. A 1987 report by Joseph Wresinski, the founder of the International Movement ATD Fourth World, submits that[4]:

---

2. For example, the Declaration and Plan of Action adopted at the World Summit for Social Development in Copenhagen in 1995 suggested that extreme poverty prevents the very poor from enjoying their fundamental rights and fulfilling their responsibilities.

3. Available at www.un.org/millenium/declaration

4. See Wresinski, J., 1987, *Grande pauvreté et précarité économique et sociale*, report adopted by the French Economic and Social Council (Journal officiel, "Avis et rapport du CES," p. 25). See also the United Nations's General Assembly Resolution 53/146 and the Human Rights Commission Resolution 1996/23 adopting the *Final Report on Human Rights and Extreme Poverty*, submitted by the Special Rapporteur, Leandro Despouy (E/CN.4/Sub.2/1996/13).

> The lack of basic security means the absence of one or more of the factors that enable individuals and families to assume basic responsibilities and to enjoy fundamental rights. Such a situation may vary in extent; its consequences can vary in gravity and may to a greater or lesser extent be irreversible. The lack of basic security leads to chronic poverty when it simultaneously affects several aspects of life, when it is prolonged and when it severely compromises people's chances of regaining their rights and of reassuming their responsibilities in the foreseeable future.

This definition underlines the continuity existing between poverty and extreme poverty, the multidimensionality of extreme poverty, its chronic character, and the inability of the very poor to exercise their rights and assume their responsibilities. Indeed, when the lack of basic securities in various areas have mutually reinforcing impacts and lead to deprivations in new areas of life, the poorest are prisoners of a vicious circle. With no basic security left as a solid foundation to rely upon, despite their efforts to fight extreme poverty, they cannot improve their condition without the help of others.

Importantly, the very poor are also socially excluded. When they are in such a situation that their chances of reassuming their responsibilities in the foreseeable future are severely compromised, they are often blamed for their lack of participation and dire living conditions, and they are often suspected of being complacent. Such misperceptions lead to further marginalization, as they are viewed as not respecting the social standards of mainstream society. As the different insecurities they face intensify and accumulate, exclusion and contempt of the poorest become worse, thus reinforcing the gap between them and the rest of society. As the very poor are excluded from participation in the decision-making processes, and more generally, in civil, social and cultural life, they are often considered ignorant and even incapable of thinking, since they have had no opportunity to gain means of expression through education.

The feeling of contempt and exclusion, severely attacking self-confidence, is deep among the poorest, whether they live in rich or poor countries. Very few people listen to them. "Instead, we impose outside interpretations on them that prevent them from reflecting on their own lives" suggested Wresinski.[5] Another important feature of extreme poverty is that people who endure it resist it; strengthening their family is one of the best ways to help them do this. Extreme poverty is destructive to family and social life. Nevertheless, the family remains a powerful means of social identification since a human being feels responsible first and foremost for the development of those closest to him or her. As Mr. Vamara Koulibaly from Côte d'Ivoire, who has been living on the streets for fifteen years, explained it: "*In Africa, family is very important. Money is not enough. The most important is family relationship. You cannot give people living on the street the love of a family. The only thing to do is to recreate links with their families. That requires much patience. You have to believe in the person. Money is not the solution. People need love and respect.*"

Overview of the Contributions in This Volume

The stories of individuals and families presented in this report, and of the projects and programs that were implemented by the International Movement ATD Fourth World to support them and enable them to express themselves, illustrate the multiple handicaps faced by

---

5. Joseph Wresinski, lecture at the Sorbonne University (Paris, 1983).

the very poor and their constant efforts to emerge from poverty. Yet in order to tell these stories and understand from the very poor themselves what it means to live in extreme poverty, attention had to be given to their voice, and to the voice of those engaged at their side.

The necessity to invest in the knowledge of the very poor and of people of action working with them is advocated in Chapter 2 by Wresinski. The chapter is a translation from French of a speech given in 1980. In this speech, Wresinski articulated a complex set of relations among different types of knowledge and action that is still worthy of attention. He invites his audience of specialists from many disciplines to think about their work in a new way. His starting point is to affirm that everyone involved—those living in extreme poverty, activists, and researchers—is a thinking human being with goals. He contends that we will see the whole picture and act effectively only when the integrity of all three parties is respected. In each case thorough understanding of a situation must come before creating concepts and designing methods. This is a fundamental lesson of epistemology, of methodology, and of ethics as well, from an original standpoint that gives specific insights. Wresinski himself experienced living in extreme poverty. He endured extreme poverty as a child born in France from migrant parents. Later, when he was a priest, he lived for ten years with the inhabitants of a shantytown close to Paris until all of them were offered new housing. With the inhabitants of this shantytown, he founded the International Movement ATD Fourth World that later spread to many countries. At the same time, together with a Dutch diplomat, he founded an Office of Social Research that later became the Research and Training Institute of this movement. His point of view is that of a man trained in the very harsh school of destitution and exclusion, who became a listened-to spokesman of the poorest at national and international levels.

Wresinski's approach opens up new possibilities. The poorest are given the chance to develop their thinking and make it known to the wider society. Activists have the chance to forge innovative partnerships. Researchers can produce work that is both rigorous and likely to make a practical difference. His hope is, of course, that the three autonomous parties will find ways to talk with one another. When they do so the field is expanded and things change for everyone. This is also the main message of Chapter 3 by Godinot, which reproduces the comments provided by the International Movement ATD Fourth World on a draft of the *World Development Report 2004: Making Services Work for Poor People*. Attention is given by Godinot to both the content of the report and to its knowledge-building process. Referring to the classification of three different types of knowledge proposed by Wresinski, Godinot argues that much more should be done to encourage truly participatory research with the very poor so that their voice can be better taken into account in policymaking.

The following chapters in this report are narratives of case studies of participatory work with very poor families led by members of the Fourth World Movement in both developing and developed countries. The setting of Chapter 4 is a Tananarive neighborhood in Madagascar with around 6,000 inhabitants living in precarious and densely-populated dwellings; only a few drinking fountains, no toilets, and flooding during the rainy season render hygiene almost non-existent. The parents have unstable jobs in the informal economy and with a surprising amount of inventiveness and energy try to provide their children with an education. In 1991, the International Movement ATD Fourth World, together with parents, launched a dual program to promote health care (which went on to last for ten years) and knowledge sharing (which is still ongoing). At the beginning, relations between the inhabitants and the health care services were shaped by a lack of understanding and fear, with inhabitants resorting to the ancestral knowledge of traditional medicine and health care staff reacting mostly according to the norms of Western medicine. After several years of work allowing the parents' capabilities to be appreciated and strengthened, dialog was made possible. This meant that new paths could be opened based on greater understanding and mutual respect.

Chapter 5 tells the story of how the Fourth World Movement's team encountered and learned from the very poor in Tanzania. When the team first arrived in the country, its mission was summed up in two challenges: "When we find the friends of the poorest of the poor, we want to learn from their experience. When we find the poorest of the poor who have no friends, we want to find friends with them." The chapter shows that reaching the poorest is difficult for at least two reasons. First, the poorest tend to be hidden. The movement's member working with poor youth in Tanzania was on his way to work one day when he discovered a group of families whose existence was ignored by others. They lived in shipwrecks that had been left on a beach to be sold later as scrap. Only at low tide was it possible to reach these people. These families were hidden to society, unknown to local organizations. Second, even when the very poor have been located, it is not easy to involve them in development projects, because of their high degree of social exclusion. The chapter reveals that in the past young adolescents would work in the old fish market of the town, doing odd jobs, such as cleaning fish, helping the fish sellers or collecting firewood, which provided them with just enough money for a small meal. However, when a development project that consisted of building a new and modern fish market was implemented, the vendors and workers were not consulted in the planning phase and it was revealed at the end that only half of them would be allowed to work within the new market. Now, a number of poor vendors and market workers who earned their meager livelihoods in the old market are without jobs. This does not mean that building the modern fish market was a bad idea—it rather means that unless special efforts are made to consult the very poor, they may suffer from programs and projects which have, overall, a beneficial impact on a community or society.

In Chapter 6, the focus shifts to the experience of the Fourth World Movement's teams in three Latin American countries: Guatemala, Peru, and Bolivia. This chapter provides contributions from these three teams. The Peru team focuses on its street library activities, the objective of which is to improve access to knowledge and education for poor children. The Guatemala team shares insights from the life of Doña Elena's family and children, as a way to better understand the difficulties which the very poor are confronted with and how they cope with these difficulties. The Bolivia team describes some activities from the Tapori network that aims to promote a better understanding among children from different socio-economic backgrounds. A key theme of this chapter is that action on the ground with very poor families and the participatory knowledge on extreme poverty acquired through this action reinforce each other.

As well as chapters based on case studies in developing countries, we have included in this report two case studies from developed countries. This is based on a conviction that many of the difficulties encountered by the very poor, and many of the lessons that can be learned from a close partnership with them are similar in both types of country.

Chapter 7 tells the story of a seminar which took place in November 2000 on unleashing the hidden potential of very poor children in the United States. In underprivileged schools, parents and teachers alike are under a great deal of pressure. What too often results is that everyone tries to find someone else to blame. Parents hope desperately that their children will not repeat their own school failures, and when they see their children struggling in school they often lash out at the teachers. Teachers are often ill-prepared to deal with conditions they find in high poverty schools, and teachers in these schools are often less trained and less experienced than teachers in other schools. In these circumstances, teachers can accuse the parents of their students of being bad parents, of not even caring about their children's education. In the face of these conflicting accusations the ones who suffer most are the children. Yet, the "Unleashing Hidden Potential" seminar showed that it is possible for people from very different backgrounds and very different perspectives to put aside their differences and seriously try to work together for the benefit of children.

Finally, Chapter 8 reproduces the synthesis of a report with the same title published by the *Service de Lutte Contre la Pauvreté, la Précarité et l'Exclusion Sociale du Centre pour l'Egalité des Chances et la Lutte Contre le Racisme* (Center for Equality of Opportunity and the War on Racism) in Brussels. The objective of the report was to conduct indepth work with families living in extreme poverty on how indicators for assessing poverty could be improved in Belgium. The report resulted from a two-year program that gathered 23 participants, including 12 who live in poverty chosen from Belgian NGOs that give the poor a chance to express their opinions. The other participants were academics, representatives of various government bodies and institutions, and the pedagogical team. The chapter provides insights on how poverty indicators could be improved to better reflect the reality of the life of the poor.

Seminar at the World Bank to Discuss the Issue of Extreme Poverty

Several of the contributions gathered in this volume were presented at a seminar on extreme poverty organized at the World Bank on October 19, 2005. On the Bank's side, participants included among others Luca Barbone, Director for Poverty Reduction, Steen Lau Jorgensen, Director for Social Development, Katherine Marshall, Director for the Development Dialogue on Values and Ethics, and Deepa Narayan, Senior Advisor and task manager of the Bank's multi-country Moving Out of Poverty study. The objective of the seminar was to better understand the life of the poor, what is needed in order to reach them, and how attacking extreme poverty represents a challenge for the Bank.

The seminar was opened with testimonies from a delegation of families living in extreme poverty across the world. This delegation had come earlier that week to represent the very poor at a meeting held at the United Nations on the occasion of October 17, the United Nations-recognized International Day for the Eradication of Poverty. Box 1 presents one of the testimonies prepared by the delegation, from a delegate from Latin America.

After the presentation of testimonies by families living in poverty, the first part of the seminar focused on ways to learn from the very poor. Staff members from the Fourth World Movement who wrote the life stories of two families in poverty, one in Burkina Faso and one in Peru, presented these life stories. These family monographs are based on several years of work with the families involved and on a close collaboration with them in writing their stories. In Burkina Faso, the focus was on Paul, a youth who lived for several years

---

Box 1.1: A Delegation of Families in Poverty is Received at the World Bank

---

"My name is María Teresa Gonzáles. I want to share with you the experiences of families in my country. The lack of stable work and housing means that it is difficult to enroll our children in school. Often the parents have to wake up at two o'clock in the morning to queue up at school, only to be told that there are no places for their children. That is the struggle of the families which can't afford to send their children to school, not because they don't want to, but because they are not able to.

One of my friends, Doña María Mercedes, is a single mother with five children. Her family has always been discriminated against and rejected by others. The oldest children have always worked to help bring food into the house. When he was seventeen her son Yoli had his first child, which was difficult for Doña Maria. Despite the extra work she didn't give up. Even though she is not well from having to fight daily to feed the household, no one acknowledges her struggle to keep the family together. Poverty and the lack of opportunity destroy and separate families. If she did not love her children, she would not be able to do all that she does. No one gives her a hand. She feels impotent when she sees her children wandering about. Juan passed third grade but his brothers and sisters did not. When you are hungry you cannot learn. María Mercedes' life is difficult and she needs friendship, not just additional material help. She needs someone to stand beside her to face those who judge and look down on her.

The families live in poverty but they do work. Policies have to be made with the families, creating a common bond together. A right fulfilled allows other rights to be fulfilled. A right violated leads to the violation of other rights."

This testimony was given by Ms. Gonzáles during the opening session of a seminar on extreme poverty organized at the World Bank on October 19, 2005. Ms. Gonzáles was part of a delegation of families living in poverty from Guatemala, Haiti, the Philippines, Tanzania and the United States that had met two days earlier with United Nations Secretary General Kofi Anan, on the occasion of the International Day for the Eradication of Poverty on October 17th. At the World Bank, the delegation met among others with Katherine Marshall, Director for the Development Dialogue on Values and Ethics, and with Jean-Louis Sarbib, Senior Vice President for Human Development.

---

in the streets of Burkina Faso. In Peru, the focus was on the Rojas-Paucar family that migrated from rural areas to Cuzco. These life stories provide a unique perspective on what the poor must go through in their daily life and how they cope with deprivation. After a presentation of these monographs, the discussion shifted to ways of making services work for poor people. Many factors prevent the very poor from using services that would make a difference in their life. This includes lack of physical access as well as lack of affordability. In addition, cultural and behavioral issues also play an important role in reducing the take-up of social services by the very poor. For example, a mutual relation of trust and understanding, normally non-existent, must be developed between the very poor and the institutions and individuals willing to serve them. This was illustrated with the cases studies on health services in Madagascar and schools in the United States presented in this volume (see chapters 4 and 8).

The second part of the seminar was devoted to recent World Bank initiatives that have the potential of informing us on what is required to fight extreme poverty, as well as to a discussion of future initiatives that could broaden the Bank's work in this area. A number of research programs have been recently implemented by the World Bank on areas that deal directly with poverty reduction. Task managers from these programs presented their findings to the extent that they do provide insights on what is needed to attack extreme poverty, and provided suggestions on what additional work would be needed to better understand priorities for attacking extreme poverty.

Finally, the last session of the seminar was devoted to an assessment of the implications of the discussions held during the day for the work of the World Bank, the Fourth World Movement, and other organizations towards the reduction of extreme poverty, with an emphasis of the type of knowledge that is required to inform this work. Seminar participants agreed that helping the very poor to emerge from poverty requires not only extra public resources, effort, and time, but also a broader approach to development policy. This again makes it important to learn from the very poor how they cope with multiple deprivations and what is needed from their point of view to attack extreme poverty.

Conclusion: Where Do We Go from Here?

One of the main findings from the October 2005 seminar mentioned above and from the contributions gathered in this volume is that the very poor should not only be taken into account, in fact they should be given priority if they are to take advantage of development projects. This is because they are in the worst situation, with the weakest capabilities to improve their daily life without the help of others. Many obstacles hinder the participation of the poorest in projects and services designed for their benefit. The preoccupation with daily survival requires all of their energy and attention. Perhaps even more significant is the fact that it is often too shameful, too painful, and too terrifying for the poorest to access services, especially those that address only their deprivations, rather than their aspirations. Indeed, the projects which are the most successful in reaching the poorest tend to be based on the aspirations they carry deep inside of them but often have difficulty expressing.

Today, many actions undertaken for reducing poverty fail to reach the very poor. Often the poorest are so excluded that they seem out of reach. This exclusion also means that their situation and their efforts to emerge from poverty will not be known to an outsider. For the outsider to acquire an indepth knowledge of the very poor and build projects with them, tools and commitments are needed. Proximity is necessary for acquiring a genuine knowledge of their aspirations. Yet, for proximity to work, the very poor need a clear understanding of the intentions of those who want to help them.

The lessons learned from the case studies presented in this volume have implications for grassroots organizations working with the very poor, governments, and even international financial organizations. Three areas of emphasis can be highlighted here[6]:

■ A first issue is the temporal dimension of programs and policies. Working with the extreme poor requires a long-term process, not one-shot interventions. Extreme poverty programs and projects will not work if there is no participation of the very poor in the interpretation and transformation of their reality. This in turn requires building the capacity of the extreme poor for transforming their existing knowledge

---

6. The three areas of emphasis highlighted here were suggested by Estanislao Gacitua-Mario.

into a powerful creative force that will break down their dependence, allowing the construction of new social relations between them and with others. What is therefore needed is the building of capacities over a long period of time. One potential solution in practice would be to think about programmatic approaches in which as the groups targeted by a program or project move along, and when certain preestablished benchmarks are met, the project can then evolve into another stage and type of investments.

- Following from the above, the types of activities that are needed in order to attack extreme poverty should not focus only on access to assets and the development of human capital. It is also important to work towards building a consensus for a new social contract in which the extreme poor (and excluded people in general) assume the role of subjects in the process of transforming and recreating the institutions that regulate decisionmaking as well as the distribution and redistribution of assets. Therefore, the types of activities that need to be supported should include programs and projects that will contribute to the development of social capital and the transformation of the social relations between excluded groups and society at large.

- In turn, this approach requires a new type of relationship between external agents (government officials, civil society volunteers, or community organizers) and the extreme poor. The case studies in this volume demonstrate that the role of external agents cannot be only to provide resources, as is for example the case for a range of recently-introduced innovative programs targeting the very poor in Latin America. There is also a need for community workers (or whatever label these persons may be given) to generate knowledge that will help the extreme poor in understanding and transforming the reality in which they live. At the project level, we also need to develop indicators of social change based on the transformation of the social relations that hinder the capacity of the extreme poor to move out of poverty, so that at least some of the projects targeting the very poor can be evaluated in part on the basis of their contribution to the systematization and expression of knowledge into organized, collective action.

To conclude, reaching the poorest requires a significant human investment not only from outsiders but also from the poorest themselves. In the same way that outsiders require training, so do the poorest, so that they can build their own expertise, and share it with others. As for the mobilization of local communities, it often begins with the detection of local groups such as community centers and schools. The dialog with the persons and institutions that will support a program for the poorest must make it clear from the beginning that partnering with the poorest does not mean entering into a short-term cooperation agreement. Because the poorest have an important role to play, they must not only be reached, but also empowered. Therefore, one could argue that the evaluation of projects aimed at reaching the very poor should be anchored in a very simple question: Has this project allowed the poorest the opportunity to advance towards greater autonomy and freedom rather than remaining in a cycle of deprivation and dependency?

PART I

Three Types of Knowledge on Poverty

CHAPTER 2

A Knowledge That Leads to Action

Joseph Wresinski[7]

Very early in the history of the International Movement ATD Fourth World, its founder declared that "knowledge [must not be] the step-child of charity." He constantly called on scientific researchers to contribute to a body of knowledge useful for the liberation of the poorest of the poor. In December 1980, Joseph Wresinski brought together an international committee of specialists at the UNESCO headquarters in Paris. The text that follows is a translation of his opening address to that committee.

As I greet you this morning within the walls of UNESCO, I realize that for nearly twenty-five years you, scholars, researchers, and the scientific communities you represent, have responded generously to calls from ATD Fourth World with faithfulness, concern, and shared hopes.... I want to remind you this morning of the role, even the duty, of all those dedicated to scientific research on poverty to make a place for the knowledge which the poor and the excluded themselves have of their condition. Beyond that, to give it pride of place because it is unique and indispensable, as well as autonomous and complementary to all other knowledge about poverty. Finally, you should help this knowledge to develop.

---

7. Joseph Wresinski was the founder of the International Movement ATD Fourth World. Entitled *La Pensée des plus pauvres dans une connaissance qui conduise au combat* this paper was initially a speech delivered in French in 1980. It was published in *Revue Quart Monde* n° 140, 1991, and then translated into English by Alice Husson, Bruno Tardieu, Xavier Louveaux, and Charles Sleeth. The translation was revised by Charles Courtney in July 2005.

To this function, you will guess, one needs to add another: that of making room for the knowledge of poverty and social exclusion which is available to those practitioners who live with the very poor and carry out projects with them, giving it the importance it deserves, and helping its development.

We have spoken to you before about these two components of global knowledge of poverty, of which yours, that of the outside observer, is the third. But in view of the work to be carried out during this three-day session and the months to follow, I take the liberty of once more clarifying some ideas our Movement has on this topic....

Academic Knowledge and Mobilization for Action

From the beginning, our Movement has held that in order to fight effectively against poverty and exclusion the following questions must be posed:

- What kind of knowledge do the poorest people need?
- What kind of knowledge do practitioners and action teams need?
- What kind of knowledge do our national societies and our international communities need?

It is fair to say that we have lived and struggled in a historical period when the answer to the question "What knowledge?" has for the most part been: properly scientific knowledge. Many expected that the knowledge best suited to the struggle, and thus to the promotion of social policies and legislative measures, would be of the same kind as that created in universities and other standard research institutions. In other words, one expected much, if not everything, from that part of knowledge available only to academics and specialists who are observers from outside the reality of poverty. This latter knowledge has been highly regarded because of its methodology, its rigor, and what was thought to be its objectivity or neutrality. These characteristics were reassuring to those who, faced with immensely complex problems which politicians construed subjectively, wished to find an objective truth, capable of guiding a clear plan of action, rooted in truth and effective for the poor.

The university came to be regarded as a guarantor of security in the face of problems so difficult to understand. It was a refuge for those who did not want to be frustrated or led into error by ideologies, whether of the dominant or the dominated. You, as well as we, have at certain times wanted to use the university in this way. And, no doubt, we weren't wrong, but we weren't totally right either.

However, contrary to what some seem to think, it is not the general discovery of the non-neutrality, the non-objectivity, of science, and particularly the human and social sciences, that proves us wrong today. Neither is it the knowledge that all science and scientific methodology are tainted with ideology that convinces us that we were not right. These are interesting problems, but, in our opinion, they are of secondary importance.

The basic problem, which we did not recognize and still haven't mastered, is that academic knowledge of poverty and social exclusion—as of all other human reality—is only a partial knowledge. We ourselves haven't said, or even sufficiently understood, that it can be only indirect and purely informative, that it lacks, by definition, a direct grasp of reality and, consequently, is not a knowledge that can mobilize people and prompt them to action.

Many of us have had the experience of being keenly disappointed when one or another of our studies had no effect. Perhaps we did not pay enough attention to the fact that academic research in the strict sense must necessarily produce an abstraction, an image of reality seen from the outside and translated into general terms that no longer include the feelings, colors, and other things that move people to take action for others.

Of comprehensive knowledge about poverty and social exclusion, knowledge meant to inform, to explain, and to lead people to action, academic research will never be more than one component among others, namely, the information component, partially explanatory, and thus lifeless. It will remain lifeless as long as two other components of knowledge are missing. These two autonomous and complementary components, which will add life and meaning, are:

- knowledge which the poor and excluded have, from their firsthand experience, of the twin realities of poverty and the surrounding world which imposes it on them; and
- the knowledge of those who work among and with these victims in places of poverty and social exclusion.

Caught in the trap of a society that believes in the supremacy of academic knowledge, our universities believed this themselves.... And when the costliest and most thorough studies and research disappeared into the drawers of politicians and administrators, we said that it was for political reasons.... This was correct, but did not allow for the possibility that the problem was not with the politicians but rather with our studies that were not the kind to prompt politicians to take action.

However, I believe that at no time did the universities admit that the political ineffectiveness of their research could be attributed to the fact that knowledge thus constructed was instructive but not convincing; nor acknowledge, moreover, that the supplements needed to convince could not come from the university researcher but solely from the poor and those who work with them.

Without Freedom of Thought, No Communication

Certainly, not all researchers ignored the two components of knowledge represented by the poor and those who work with them. However, and this is the crux of the matter, they did not regard them as autonomous components to be pursued by and for the authors themselves. Scholars quickly turned them into the object of their own research; they regarded these components as sources of information to be used for their own purposes, rather than as equally valid research projects, as supporting subjects and not objects of exploitation. They have, to some extent, subordinated these components to their own exploration as outside observers of the life of the poor and the actions undertaken with them. Thus, they have deflected a knowledge, which did not belong to them, from its own goal. More seriously, these researchers have often, unintentionally and unwittingly, upset or even paralyzed the thinking of their interlocutors. This happened essentially because they did not recognize that they were dealing with a thinking and an autonomous inquiry that followed their own path and goals. Consequently, they have not respected these goals. They have treated their research subjects as sources of information rather than as independent thinkers. This is why we have always doubted the value of the information obtained by academics.

As for communicating with the very poor, many years of observation have convinced us that even the so-called participatory observation practiced by anthropologists and ethnologists runs the danger of misusing, tampering with, and paralyzing the thinking of the poor. This is so because it is an observation for a goal external to their life situation, one that they did not choose and which they would never have defined in the same way as the investigators. Consequently, the observation is not truly participatory since the thinking of the investigators and that of the population which is the object of their observation do not pursue the same goals.

It is not a problem of method, but a question of life situation, one that cannot be resolved by adopting other methods but only by change in situation. Moreover, participant observation, which certainly will not disturb the thinking of a group in full possession of its powers of reflection and culture, runs the serious risk of disturbing the thinking of the very poor who do not master them nearly as well.

It goes without saying that a similar problem arises for the cooperation between investigators and men and women of action. These difficulties have often been analyzed. For example, it has been said that action teams have difficulty collaborating in research because they don't see the point of the project and because they are suspicious of the scrutinizing look of the researchers and of their inability to understand the human reality and chaos of everyday life. It has even been said that collaboration does not work because practitioners lack logical skills and base their action on intuitions and impressions rather than rational reflection.

There may be some truth in these explanations, but it seems to us that they do not go to the heart of the matter. The basic problem is that if practitioners are to make a valuable contribution they must be seen from the outset not as mere providers of information, but as thinkers having to pursue to the very end their own quest for knowledge, according to their own goals.

Here again we are convinced, thanks to what we have learned from many years of experience, that even social scientists who have been brought in to analyze an action and evaluate its results often run the risk of going astray. In fact, don't they often arrive when the die has already been cast and try to understand, after the fact, a situation which is totally foreign to them? They face a situation different from any they know, one fraught with unimaginable insecurity and for which they have very little feeling.

The nature and dynamics of such a situation can be grasped only to the extent that one appreciates the insecurity and shifting sands of a life of action with those in extreme poverty. One can understand such an action only to the degree in which one has participated in the development of the thinking of the action team and by adopting the objectives of that thinking.

Having said this, our purpose was not to draw attention to the weakness of academic studies resulting from problems of communication. We wanted above all to make the point that these studies all together, whatever their quality, would not be able to provide the totality of the required knowledge.

Let us turn again for a moment to the two other sources of this knowledge. In principle, they are complementary to that of the university, but they can only take shape and be fully complementary when they are autonomous and allowed to reach their final goals on their own.

The Secret Garden of the Poorest of the Poor

Let us consider for a moment the knowledge and way of thinking of the people of the Fourth World. They deal not only with their life situation but also with the environing world which traps them in poverty and with the contrast between what is and what ought to be if the weakest are no longer to be excluded.

Thinking and knowing are acts which all human beings perform, and they do them with whatever means, sophisticated or not, that life has provided. Each person thinks, knows, and strives to understand in order to achieve his or her own goal. Since their thinking is oriented to that goal, every act of thinking can become an act of personal liberation. The Fourth World Movement, on the basis of its experience in diverse areas of poverty throughout the world, can attest that every person and every group attempts to perform this act, however meager their means of thinking and analysis. All human beings and groups are researchers, seeking independence through understanding themselves and their situation so that they control their destiny rather than submitting and being afraid.

Those who think that human beings reduced to total poverty are apathetic and consequently don't think, that they retreat into dependency or the simple struggle to survive day to day, make a serious mistake. They ignore the strategies of self-defense that the poor create to escape the influence of those on whom they are dependent. They protect their own existence, which they carefully hide behind the "life" that they spread out like a curtain and "play" to create an illusion for the external observer. Finally, they ignore the desperate effort to reflect and explain of those who constantly ask themselves, "Just who am I, after all?" or who say, "They treat me like a dog, like a spineless coward, an idiot, a non-entity…. Am I really a spineless coward?" And there are those who through a painful effort of thinking constantly rise up from under their own personalities and those accusations which are so many monstrous identities heaped upon them by repeating to themselves, "But I am not a dog. I am not the idiot I am made out to be. I know things, but they will never understand."

And they are absolutely right to come to this conclusion that always emerges once the doubts have been dispelled, even though they are left totally exhausted in body and mind. Surely they "know things" that others are unlikely ever to understand or even imagine. This knowledge, not well structured to be sure, is about being condemned for life to contempt and social exclusion. It covers everything that that signifies: facts, suffering, but also the resilience and hope called forth by those facts. It also includes knowledge of the surrounding world, including certain attitudes toward the very poor that only they would know.

Even the best researchers find it difficult to imagine these things; consequently, they have a hard time formulating suitable hypotheses and questions. They find themselves facing something that they do not have the tools to master. It is so to speak the secret garden of the very poor. Entry is open only to those who change their life situation and become partners with the poor in a project which is no longer one of mere research but of liberation.

Otherwise, it is hard to imagine how those coming from another world and whose thinking is shaped by that world could gain entrance to the secret garden. And there is more. Besides not being able to enter, they would not have the right to do so.

In fact, no one has the right, even in the name of science, to hinder another's effort, perhaps clumsy but nonetheless relentless, to develop a liberating outlook. No researcher has the right to exploit the efforts of the poorest to liberate themselves in order to put them back into servitude. For it cannot be said too often that to hinder the poorest by using them as informants rather than encouraging them to develop their own thinking as a genuinely autonomous act is to enslave them. All the more so because their thinking is almost always a search for their history and identity, and they alone have direct access to an essential part of the answers. They ask themselves questions about their history and identity, much more than about their needs or even their rights, because they know, perhaps confusedly but profoundly, that it is through these questions that they will find the path to freedom.

We do not mean to say that it is always a mistake to speak to them about their rights or to question them about their needs. However, such an approach can be liberating for them only the extent that these exchanges take place within the perspective of their understanding of their historical identity, the only knowledge that can help them to be subjects and master of their rights and needs.

This has rarely been the case so far. Throughout the entire period of what was called "the War on Poverty" in the United States, we did not see a single truly historical piece of research on the lives of those who in those days were called the "hardcore" poor. Nor, even less, was there research carried out in close collaboration with the "hardcore" poor themselves.

In the European Community at last some interest is being shown in what is called persistent poverty, that is to say, poverty having an historical dimension from which would logically follow the historical identity of a "lumpen-proletariat." But this dimension or this historical identity is rarely brought out and can be developed only through an ongoing dialog with the families of the Fourth World. We are concerned because we do not see any bridges being built between the University and the Fourth World. We do see a search for ways of collecting information without having to go through a process of creating a lasting collaboration with the families concerned.

This also holds true for Great Britain, a country which we regard as exemplary because it steadfastly continued research on poverty even during the great prosperity of the 1960s. But even there, historical research does not exist. The only identity the poor have is through what they need, what they lack. This is partially attributable to the respect researchers have for the poor and their concern not to put them in a category of their own, thereby contributing to their segregation. However, is this right when we consider that their historical identity is one of immeasurable resilience and inalienable dignity? When we consider furthermore that it is an identity that carries an essential message to the whole society?

It is not our intention to criticize, much less to denigrate in any way, the sincere and intelligent efforts made by our friends from the United States, Great Britain, and Europe. Our role is simply to remind everyone what the very poor families gathered in the Fourth World Movement have taught us. To talk to them only of their needs, or of those "social indicators" which characterize them, without helping them to better understand their own history or the common traits of their lives is just another way of trapping them. It is the families themselves who call on the Movement; and their request is not, "Explain to us," but rather, "Help us to think." Some families, and they are growing in number, say, We must think, because others will never be able to understand."

Restoring Thinking, Supporting the Effort of the Fourth World to Know

We count on you academic researchers for a careful study and interpretation of what the Fourth World has taught us about its right to have its thinking and autonomous knowledge recognized. It is up to you and to us to discover how to support its effort of reflection. For, if the people of the Fourth World have shown clearly that they want to carry out their own thinking to the end, they have never said that they need no help in this undertaking. On the contrary, wherever our teams are established we hear, like a leitmotiv this request: "You, who have learned to think, teach us how to." Whether it be in Guatemala, Switzerland, New York, Bangkok, or the run-down areas of London, the poorest are calling for the presence not of "thought masters" (they see too many of them), but of competent and intelligent men and women who can teach them how to think without insinuating themselves into the thinking itself.

However, do we know enough about the tools, the methodology, and the pedagogy needed for this endeavor? I am not so sure. It is not that there are no pioneers in this area. But, a careful look at the experiments carried out in several countries leaves us with our doubts. Perhaps it is because the projects carried out in the name of one or the other of the pedagogies of "conscientization" in Latin America, India, or even Europe seemed almost without exception to leave out the poor. Whether in Indian villages of Colombia, hamlets of untouchables of India, slums of Calcutta, or a poor area of Portugal, the most impoverished inhabitants find themselves marginalized even from these projects.

Perhaps these projects raise questions for us because they transport curiously Western language and concepts all the way to the Far East and to the perched villages on the high plateaus of Bolivia far from modern civilization. Did these people invent this vocabulary strangely familiar to our Western ears: "power relations," "exploitation of man by man," "class warfare"? Would they not have chosen to speak in the words of their own civilization?

I believe that those of us here could have something to say about this question: we could bring to light the conditions required for authentic support of the thinking of the poorest; we could recognize those projects favorable to the development of an independent knowledge proper to the Fourth World. Without the knowledge that the poor possess and ought to be able to develop, university studies risk being knowledge which is much too partial and which lacks precisely what would make it life-giving and precipitate action and struggle.

Without getting into philosophy or social psychology, let us simply state the two reasons which, in the experience of the Movement, explain why only the voice of the poor is conducive to action and why all other knowledge is only supportive.

First, in a world full of good causes, appeals of less than far-reaching importance, despite what we might expect, are not going to convince our fellow citizens to make a serious commitment to sustainable action. Partial knowledge which does not go to the heart of the problem, namely the suffering and the hopes of the totally excluded, will not challenge people and call forth indispensable major commitments. It is because it never compromised its presentation of the extreme consequences of poverty that our Movement of ordinary citizens managed to take on dimensions that its modest resources could not explain.

Yet, only the very poor know these extreme consequences. They alone know all the injustice, all the denial of human rights, all the suffering due to exclusion. They alone know what must be changed in hearts and minds and in the structures and functioning of our democracies. But of all that, the conclusions of the past twenty-five years of academic studies are only a weak reflection, an abbreviated message.

Second, when we look at the totality of the message communicated by the families of the Fourth World, we can see that it is not marginal but central and essential because it tells us everything we need to know about society as it is and as it ought to be. Some of you will recall the attempts made to get that message across in the 1960s at the International Association of Sociology Forum. These efforts were repeated in the 1970s in the pilot program, "European Program of Research and Action Against Poverty." Our Movement proposed a study of the tools and conditions which would be required to enable the poorest of the poor of the European Community to speak for themselves rather than having to wait for social scientists to do it for them. Even though the proposal came at the time of the election of the European Parliament by universal franchise, governmental experts did not find the project of immediate interest.

Experience shows us that the Movement gains new members around the world only when it gives Fourth World families the floor and lets them express their own truths. We are only a non-governmental organization; yet, if we have been able to endure and expand, is it not because the message from the poorest can convince, is irrefutable because of its integrity?

Let me repeat, what matters to a Movement that is confronted every day with the harsh reality of a struggle is that our fellow-citizens hear the voices of the poor themselves, in their very own words, rather than a translation by some university study. Should we not be modest enough to admit this? Political support has been gained because people realize that our Movement makes the voices of the poor heard so that everyone can listen.

Our Committee should spend at least part of its time strengthening both the thinking of the poor, which is essential in gaining an understanding of exclusion, and their way of expressing themselves, which is essential in securing the commitment of our fellow citizens to the struggle. The issue will be brought up as early as today during our debate about the Seminar, "The Fourth World in Africa." It will come up again tomorrow during our debate on the significance of European policies on poverty in the member states of the European Union. And the issue will come up for a third time in its most crucial dimensions when the subject of alliances and partnerships in the struggle against exclusions will be broached by our friend, Professor Jona Rosenfeld.

The question is therefore relevant to all the discussions planned for this session of the Committee, but more importantly, in our opinion, it seems to be part both of the raison d'être of this Committee and of its long-term goals. This is the reason why we felt it appropriate to bring it up right at the start of this conference.

An Action That Thinks and Communicates Itself

Is it necessary to expand on our previous comments about the necessary independence of the knowledge gained by people of action? What we have just said about the rights of the Fourth World in this regard obviously applies to them as well. A necessarily unique way of thinking must be built on the action, the uncertainties, the stalemates, the reactions and changes, as well as the new ideas and actions that are called forth. This thinking needs to be supported by competent outsiders while remaining autonomous and free to pursue its own objectives.

Those responsible for action need this thinking in order to be able to fulfill their commitments. Equally obvious is that Fourth World families need to have alongside them teams that are free and able to think independently.

Of course, as is the case for the poorest of the poor, practitioners and their activities can become a topic of academic research. One can even attempt, as we have mentioned, to evaluate the results of their efforts. While admitting that there exist very interesting studies in this area, we have reservations. Our first concern is that these academic studies attempt to capture the action from the outside and cannot replace the knowledge that the action can and should have of itself, for itself. This is an area that remains virtually inaccessible to social scientists for the same reasons which put the reality experienced by the poorest of the poor beyond their reach.

The knowledge of practitioners, the third kind of knowledge mentioned earlier, is an essential component of the comprehensive and stimulating knowledge that we need. The wider world needs it to be able to take action. It needs examples of citizens who are committed to action. It needs to listen to them as much as it needs to listen to scholars teaching.

Besides listening to the very poor, is it not the stories of actions told by the actors that prompt people to action? These stories can instill in others the desire and the courage, in their turn, to undertake new actions.

Here again, academic researchers could render an invaluable service by committing themselves to value and support this knowledge rather than appropriating it for their own purposes.

A Committee Ready for Action

We believe that the very poor point to a key role for university researchers. They can bring together academics, people from the Fourth World, and teams of practitioners for a successful collaboration in which each partner remains free. Together the three groups can value, support, and assist in developing new approaches to knowledge of poverty. This Committee is in position to contribute to this effort.

Whereas academics can do other valuable things, at this time this work appears to be the most necessary and innovative. That is the case, provided that we all agree that this Committee, into which we have put our energy and hope, should be not be just a wise and intelligent reminder of the extreme poverty in this world, but rather a leader calling our fellow citizens to action.

CHAPTER 3

Making Services Work for Very Poor People: Comments on the World Development Report 2004

Xavier Godinot[8]

This chapter provides an edited version of comments provided by the International Movement ATD Fourth World on a draft of the World Development Report 2004: Making Services Work for Poor People (WDR, hereafter). Attention is given to both the content of the report and to its knowledge building process. Referring to the classification of three different types of knowledge proposed by Wresinski (see Chapter 2), a key message from this chapter is that much more should be done to encourage truly participatory research with the very poor so that their voice be better taken into account in policymaking.

The draft of the WDR dated April 2003 has evolved substantially, as compared to previous versions, showing evidence that comments by many NGOs and other stakeholders have been taken into account. The analysis of the strong and weak aspects of market and state service delivery concerning health, education, water, and sanitation is better balanced than in previous drafts where market failures and state successes were underestimated.

---

8. Xavier Godinot is the representative of the International Movement ATD Fourth World to the International Financial Institutions. This paper was reviewed by Jean-Marie Anglade, Jason French, Jean-Pierre Gollé, Xavier Louveaux, Diana Skelton, Thierry Viard, Susie Devins (Deputy Director General) and Eugen Brand (Director General). Editing was done for this report by Quentin Wodon. The World Development Report commented upon, comprising about 400 pages, was dated April 27th or 29th, 2003, depending on chapters. However, all references are to the final version. The views expressed in this chapter are those of the authors, and they do not necessarily represent those of the World Bank, its Executive Directors, or the countries they represent.

The report clearly states that while economic growth is essential, it is far from being sufficient to meet the Millenium Development Goals and to succeed in the fight against poverty. If countries continue at the present rate of progress, universal primary education completion will come only after 2030 for South Asia and not at all in the foreseeable future for Sub-Saharan Africa. Because economic growth alone is not enough, the international community has committed itself to increase the transfer of resources from developed to developing countries. If the Millenium Development Goals are to be met, an increase in external resources and more effective use of internal and external resources are indeed urgently needed. Donors must better coordinate and honor their side of the Monterrey agreement by assisting performing countries.

The main message of the report is that services are often failing poor people in access, in quantity, and in quality. However, they can be made to work for poor people by putting the poor people themselves at the center of service delivery, by helping them improve their ability to monitor and discipline service providers and amplify their voice in policymaking and in the political process, and by increasing the incentives to service providers to better serve poor people. "Governments and donors frequently neglect the possible role of poor clients in sustaining better services.… Neither governments nor donors are accustomed to asking the poor for advice."[9]

The report also clearly demonstrates the huge disparities in access to services—health, education, water, energy, and sanitation—between rich and poor people. Most often, those who need the most get the least, pay the most and lack the power to get results. Four main reasons explain why services are failing poor people: public spending on health and education is typically enjoyed by the non-poor; when it is reallocated towards the poor, intermediaries seize the money and divert it from the front line providers; the incentives for service providers (such as doctors, nurses teachers) to properly perform their work are often very weak; there is often a lack of demand from poor people due to fees and physical/social distance between them and service providers.

The report considers a Human Rights approach, emphasizing equality in dignity and equality in opportunity, a valuable complement to economic analysis. It consequently states that Governments are responsible for making services work for poor people, since human rights are the responsibility of States and citizens. We welcome this breakthrough about human rights that NGOs had been requesting for a long time, and hope that future reports will build on it. Because the poor have little political voice, public services targeted at the poor are very likely to be substandard services, used only by those who have no other choice. As Human Rights are for all, we think that services must be made to work for all, including the poorest people.

We acknowledge that given the wide range of services and country circumstances discussed in the report, it is impossible to claim that a particular level of user fees or none at all is appropriate in every case. Yet, we urge the World Bank to take a firm stance against user fees for basic health and primary education services in most circumstances, except where there is an overwhelming and uncontested evidence of support for such fees. Even in rich countries where access to school is supposedly free, mandatory expenses such as books, schoolbags and outings are very hard to meet for poor families. The need to plan for and

---

9. WDR 2004 p. 64.

fully finance the abolition of fees for basic health and primary education will probably require a substantial increase in donor support.

The last chapter of the report "Donors and service reform" is one of the most courageous and helpful, because it puts donor countries—those who run the World Bank—and the Bank itself in front of their responsibilities. Donors supply 20 percent or more of the public resources in more than 60 countries, and more than 40 percent of public resources in at least 30 poor countries, such as Bolivia, Madagascar, and Tanzania. The report suggests that the way in which donors provide their aid is highly significant and that it often weakens the recipient's internal system and undermines its capacity to deliver services.

In fact, aid remains much more donor-driven than demand-driven by people living in poverty. The fact that Tanzanian government officials have to prepare about 2,000 reports of different kinds to donors, and they receive more than 1,000 donor delegations each year makes distressing reading. It is equally disturbing to note that many World Bank projects were implemented by setting up autonomous units staffed with people who sometimes were paid 12 to 24 times the salary available to the highest paid senior economist in the civil service of the country itself. A study of about 100 World Bank projects in the Latin America and Caribbean region shows that project implementation units, which hijack the countries' elite, have no significant positive impact on project outcomes while the likely sustainability of results clearly suffered.[10] A parallel study in the Eastern Europe and Central Asia region produced similar findings. There is an urgent need to reform donors' aid, including that of the Bank itself.

The Nature of Chronic Poverty and the Challenge of Its Eradication

The WDR's definition of "poor people" is very broad, because it includes people in households living below a particular consumption threshold, such as US$1 or US$2 a day, but also people experiencing any of the many dimensions of poverty and those at risk of poverty. "So poor people can be seen as the 'working class'…. Even in middle-income countries the 'poor' includes a large part of the population…[which] cannot insulate itself from the consequences of failures of public services."[11] Yet if some economists define extreme poverty as the situation of people whose income is less than one dollar per day, the very poor do not do so. In our long-term commitment with people living in extreme poverty in various parts of the world, we have never heard such a materialistic definition of poverty expressed by them. Therefore we think it necessary to investigate more deeply what poverty is. A grassroots testimony, recently reported by Koralie, a full-time volunteer of the International Movement ATD Fourth World working in Madagascar, will enable us to show how we tackle the issue:

> Though Angeline is 18 months old, her weight is only 5 kilos. On the way to the nutrition
> center, her father, Mr. René, tells Koralie that a doctor advised him to give his daughter
> minced meat, which he cannot afford. In the nutrition center, the doctor asks many questions

---

10. WDR 2004, pp. 205–6. A fierce denunciation of this World Bank practice in Western Africa can be found in Aminata D. Traoré, *L'Etau, l'Afrique dans un monde sans frontières*, Actes Sud, 1999, 185 pages.

11. WDR 2004, p. 20.

about the age of the child, the vaccines she received, the situation of the family. Mr. René tries to answer as best he can. Then the doctor asks how he feeds his daughter. Very worried, Mr. René looks at Koralie and answers, "I give her minced meat and very soft rice." Then the doctor makes the gesture of handing the toddler back and says mockingly: "If you can afford to give her minced meat every day, we need not welcome her here." Deeply humiliated, Mr. René asked Koralie what he should say. He must once more bring out into the open the humiliating truth that allows his child to be registered in the center. While receiving the baby, the staff comments on her disastrous state.

Within a few weeks, Angeline puts on weight. She is allowed to come back home providing that she keeps in close touch with the center. Mr. René has to take her to the center, in addition to taking care of his six children since his wife is disabled. Getting in touch with the center remains a humiliating and daunting experience that he finds difficult to cope with. A few months later, Angeline is again wasting away and soon dies.

This story shows in striking terms how the world of the doctor and that of Mr. René are in conflict. In some ways, it is an archetype of the relationship the very poor often have with mainstream society, and many developing countries have with donor countries. It is clear that Mr. René on the one hand and the doctor on the other share a common goal: the preoccupation of the ill health and wasting away of Angeline. When he walks with Koralie, Mr. René says clearly that he cannot afford to give his daughter minced meat. How is he then led to tell the doctor the reverse, which results in his losing any credibility in the doctor's opinion and probably in his own opinion as well? He does not intend to lie, but the question of the doctor touches the raw nerve of his inability to provide for the basic needs of his daughter and of his fear of the institution the doctor represents.

The fear he feels leads him to hear in the doctor's question: "Are you a good father to your daughter, a good partner for promoting her health?" He replies by introducing himself as a good father, very worried by his daughter's health, repeating the words he heard from other doctors. Indeed, talking about Angeline's food with the doctor is very tricky, because Mr. René knows too well how much he fails in providing her with what she needs despite his desperate efforts. This doctor is very busy, treating hundreds of undernourished children. Will he make himself available to listen to the awful deprivations, which cause Angeline's starvation? Will he agree to disrupt his routine so as to listen to and support Mr. René? Koralie understood from Mr. René that minced meat is beyond his means, because unlike the doctor she is closer to him; she knows the trouble he has with his children and is there to support him.

In such a situation, how is extreme poverty best defined? Is it Mr. René's persistent lack of basic securities, demonstrated by his child's malnutrition, his illiteracy, his living in a small shack with his family and by many other deprivations as well? Is it rather his inability to have access to his rights and to assume his responsibilities, as suggested in a comprehensive definition used by international bodies, which underlines the link between the lack of basic securities and extreme poverty?[12] Is it a deprivation of basic capabilities and

---

12. The *Final Report on Human Rights and Extreme Poverty*, submitted by the Special Rapporteur, Leandro Despouy, (E/CN.4/Sub.2/1996/13) and adopted by the UN General Assembly Resolution 53/146 and UN Human Rights Commission Resolution 1996/23 proposed the following definition: "*The lack of basic security means the absence of one or more of the factors that enable individuals and families to assume basic responsibilities and to enjoy fundamental rights. Such a situation may vary in extent; its consequences can vary in gravity and may to a greater or lesser extent be irreversible. The lack of basic security leads to chronic*

a lack of freedom, as argued by Amartya Sen?[13] Over all, is it not the failure in the relationship of two people who have the same goals but whose relationship is distorted by shame on the one hand and blame on the other? These questions lead to several comments.

First, we consider it very important to make a distinction between people living in poverty and people living in extreme poverty, since the former are often excluded from development programmes that benefit the latter. We draw the attention of World Bank staff and other international bodies to the unexpected potential side effects of the Millennium Development Goals (MDGs) on the very poor. The targets of halving in fifteen years time the proportion of people whose income is less that one dollar a day or the proportion of people who suffer from hunger are two benchmarks towards the goal of "eradicating extreme poverty." Yet these targets inevitably raise the question: what about the other half? Are they going to be better off or worse off at the end of that period? Grassroots examples suggest that the situation of the first half may very well be improved at the expense of the other half that may be impoverished.[14] If this were to happen worldwide, increasing the already large gap between the very poor and mainstream society, it would be a disaster. UNICEF was one of the first United Nations Agencies to state as early as 1989 that 20 percent of the people for whom its programmes were designed were not reached, which led them to produce a study in partnership with ATD Fourth World, *Reaching the poorest*, which provides useful guidelines for thought and action.[15]

Second, if the scale of issues related to extreme poverty is undoubtedly very different in rich and poor countries, is their nature so different? "What do families living in poverty in my country mostly refuse about their situation?" wonders a Fourth World delegate who has been living in poverty for many years in one of the richest European countries[16]:

> They refuse to be treated as if they were nothing. They refuse to accept that they cannot be good parents for their own children, that they have nothing to offer them, and that they are in fact considered as a threat to them. Government policy is not designed with this in mind, except to reduce the cost to the State. Many of the actions and programs concerning the poor turn into oppression for them.

What people in extreme poverty mostly refuse about their situation, whichever country they are from, is to be treated "like animals"[17] or "as if they were nothing." This common feature makes us question the fact that poverty in rich countries is not better taken into account in the WDR 2004. This would have had two benefits. Firstly, to remind rich countries

---

poverty when it simultaneously affects several aspects of life, when it is prolonged and when it severely compromises people's chances of regaining their rights and of reassuming their responsibilities in the foreseeable future" This definition was proposed in a report by Joseph Wresinski entitled *"Grande pauvreté et précarité économique et sociale"*, adopted by the French Economic and Social Council in 1987 (Journal officiel, "Avis et rapport du CES", p. 25). Comments on this definition can be found in Quentin Wodon (ed.), *Attacking Extreme Poverty: Learning from the Experience of the International Movement ATD Fourth World*, World Bank Technical Paper n° 502, May 2001, pages 16 to 22.

13. Amartya Sen, *Development as freedom,* Oxford University Press, 1999.

14. Xavier Godinot, *Contribution to the Poverty day, 17th October 2002 at the World Bank,* available at www.atd-fourthworld.org

15. ATD Fourth World and UNICEF, *Reaching the poorest,* 1999, 124 pages.

16. Contribution from a Fourth World delegate at the International Orientation Committee of ATD Fourth World at Méry sur Oise, France, in January 2003.

17. "They treat us like animals" says a patient in West Africa, reported in WDR 2004 Overview, p. 4.

that they have failed to eradicate extreme poverty within their borders despite the fact that they have the necessary economic resources to do so. Recognizing this failure and illustrating how their services fail poor people would have helped them to be more humble with developing countries, to consider them more like partners who share similar concerns rather than as beneficiaries of aid. Secondly, this would have helped wealthy countries to define the real nature of extreme poverty by recognizing what is wrong in their development and distribution process, and the fact that they lack the proper knowledge and the moral, political, or civic strength to make services work for the very poor. How could it be otherwise that even in rich countries, there are still two-tiered systems in housing and sanitation, education and health?

The international social and economic order should also be challenged in the WDR 2004 so as to give poor people a better chance. Aminata Traoré, a former minister of culture in Mali, writes[18]:

> Africa is being emptied at the same time of its raw materials, its capital, its valid labour and its brains. Just add to that picture the plunder of art objects to get an idea of the huge amount of resources taken out of this continent. Just imagine the possible inversion of these trends to have an idea of what Africa could become.

Finally, one must recall that at the request of our Movement, the United Nations General Assembly decided in December 1992 to declare the 17th of October a World Day to overcome extreme poverty. Since then, the many events that have taken place on this day have contributed to raise awareness of extreme poverty as a violation of human rights. The following sentence is engraved in stone in many places around the world and at the United Nations Headquarters in New York: "Wherever men and women are condemned to live in extreme poverty, human rights are violated. To come together to ensure that these rights be respected is our solemn duty" (signed by Joseph Wresinski, founder of ATD Fourth World). Despite this progress, we deeply regret that the recognition of poverty as a violation of human rights is not yet reflected in the mandate and the operations of the Bretton Woods institutions.[19]

The Uncertainty of Statistics on Extreme Poverty

The WDR 2004, as in other years, displays many statistics on poverty. Surprisingly, their reliability is not often questioned. We think it would be misleading to consider these statistics as flawless. Leandro Despouy mentioned in a Report on Human Rights and Extreme Poverty[20] four factors that may affect the reliability of statistics on extreme poverty.

Firstly, the poorest people are not contacted when statistics are gathered. Even in industrialized countries which have the technical and financial means to gather meaningful

---

18. Aminata Traoré, *Le viol de l'imaginaire*, Actes Sud/Fayard, 2002, p. 96.

19. Some small improvements are listed in the chapter 4 "Dialogue with the I.M.F." and the World Bank of the report "Human Rights and Extreme Poverty" by A-M. Lizin, independent expert to the UN Human Rights Commission (E/CN.4/2001/54)

20. *Final Report on Human Rights and Extreme Poverty*, submitted by the Special Rapporteur, Leandro Despouy. (E/CN.4/Sub.2/1996/13) and adopted by the UN General Assembly Resolution 53/146, paragraphs 48 to 74.

statistics, the statistics often do not take into account the poorest section of the population: homeless people are not covered; nomads, political refugees, illegal immigrants, and inhabitants of shanty towns are almost inevitably underrepresented. We are witness to the fact that even in developed countries, and more so in developing countries, many extremely poor people do not even appear on the civil registers. How can they be represented in surveys based on national censuses? A second reason is that the parameters used are often inappropriate. This is particularly true when the household income is precarious and fluctuates daily. Yet technical difficulties are not the whole story. A third reason is a lack of interest in and regard for the poorest section of the population. In industrialized countries whose statistical coverage is the most advanced, we met experts on poverty who considered it too expensive and too difficult to include the very poor in their surveys on poverty. Last but not least, there is a risk of manipulation of the data: this is common knowledge in regard to unemployment figures, but this is also true for poverty lines that are, inevitably, somewhat arbitrary.

Experts from different bodies recently challenged the World Bank statistical methodology. The Least Developed Countries Report 2002 published by the UN Conference on Trade and Development (UNCTAD) questioned the World Bank's poverty estimates. These estimates, which use the $1 and $2 a day poverty lines, are based on survey data of household income or consumption. UNCTAD used instead national-accounts-consistent poverty estimates and concluded that the extent of poverty in Africa, particularly sub-Saharan Africa, had been seriously understated.[21] For instance, according to the World Bank, a Tanzanian national lived on $814 average annual income in 1991, whereas according to UNCTAD, this average income was in fact less than $300. UNCTAD insisted that there is an urgent need to improve poverty statistics, which should be done by helping the least developed countries improve their capacities for national accounts as well as household surveys.

Two academics of Columbia University in New York, Sanjay G. Reddy and Thomas W. Pogge, dispute the Bank poverty lines, claiming massive flaws in its procedures. They argue that the Bank's "estimates are flawed due to three related but distinct types of significant conceptual errors, which make it impossible to use them to identify with any reasonable degree of accuracy the level, distribution and trend of global poverty." Martin Ravallion of the Bank replied by arguing: "Reddy and Pogge have oversimplified the problem of measuring poverty in the world and exaggerated the supposed faults in the Bank's methods." Yet the latter insist that the World Bank global income poverty estimates do not stand up to serious scrutiny and other researchers contest the Bank's methods as well.[22]

While we are not experts in this debate, we must point out that the threefold nature of the World Bank, which grants loans, designs policies and carries out research, contributes to give higher weight to its own figures, to the detriment of other analyses. Muhammad Yunus, a former professor of economics and famous founder of the micro-credit Grameen Bank in Bangladesh, contended that in his country, "political leaders and academics swear

21. UNCTAD, *The Least Developed Countries, 2002 report*. The whole report can be downloaded from www.unctad.org.

22. See Thomas W. Pogge and Sanjay G. Reddy, *How not to count the poor?* This paper is available on www.socialanalysis.org as well as Martin Ravallion's reply, authors' reply to Ravallion and many other papers related to the controversy.

by the figures displayed in donors' documents, even when they personally know that these figures are inaccurate"[23] just because they want to get loans which rarely benefit the poor.

These disputes between experts may affect the evaluation of the Millennium Development Goals, because targets of precise figures have been set. We think that a most helpful way to improve statistics on poverty would be to help developing countries improve their own capacities and at the same time to develop in all countries a dialog between statisticians who have technical expertise and people living in poverty who have life expertise, so as to try and find a consensus between them on what defines poverty and chronic poverty and how to measure them. "The Social Protection Committee recognizes the importance of increasing the involvement of excluded people in the development of indicators and the need to explore more effective means of giving a voice to the excluded" states the *Report on Indicators in the Field of Poverty and Social Exclusion,* which was adopted by the European Employment and Social Affairs Council of Ministers in December 2001.[24] As a followup to this recommendation, Belgian NGOs have launched a two-year research-action program about indicators on poverty, which links people living in poverty with academics and representatives of different administrations. The program is funded by the federal and regional authorities.

The Knowledge Building Process of the WDR Report

A grassroots antipoverty activist in Senegal told us recently,[25]

> Poverty has become a singsong, everybody speaks about it in my country. Yet in villages, people do not even have water to drink. We need long-term programs that would result in self-responsibility and autonomy. This would require getting to know the concerns of the people, lending a hand, walking alongside them. Yet this is not the way program designers view it: they think it would be too long. As a rule, this has not yet been experimented in our countries. People keep on thinking that entering into an alliance with the poor will make them poor.

Two years ago, an international working group which focused on the development process promoted by multilateral institutions, including World Bank staff, stated that over the past two decades, the approach on development centered on the importance of economic growth and argued that the central role played by development experts had contributed to the destruction of many society and community structures. "It has brought with it the imposition of cultural norms of the development institutions and their agents, as though these had some kind of universal validity."[26] The International Monetary Fund and the World Bank answered these criticisms by replacing in 1999 the former Structural Adjustment Programs with the Poverty Reduction and Growth Facility, aimed at promoting anti-poverty strategies, country ownership, and the participation of civil society.

23. Muhammad Yunus, *Vers un monde sans pauvreté,* éditions J. C. Lattès, 1997, pages 32–33.

24. See http://europa.eu.int/comm/employment_social/news/2002/jan/report_ind_en.pdf.

25. Contribution from an ATD Fourth World member at the International Orientation Committee of ATD Fourth World at Méry sur Oise, France, in January 2003.

26. World Faith Development Dialogue, *Cultures, spirituality and development,* July 2001, p. 4. Katherine Marshall, director for the development dialogue on values and ethics at the World Bank, was a member of the group. Web site: www.wfdd.org.uk.

Whether these initiatives will reach their goals remains to be seen. Yet, it is recognized inside the international financial institutions that the transformation they are trying to effect "requires some basic behavioral changes in the way various large international institutions, country governments and civil society interact in formulating politically, economically and sociologically complex programs."[27] We will argue that these behavioral changes include recognizing different types of knowledge. We will then underline some limits of the WDR 2004 building process and finally insist on the huge lack of real participatory research on poverty.

Recognizing Different Types of Knowledge

The French philosopher of science Michel Serres wrote a few years ago: "Human sciences are the property of very few people. Knowledge, culture and science currently contribute to inequality, competition, division and consequently produce misery as well." Serres considered this "the biggest contemporary issue"[28] and stated that "Not until destitution gets into science and culture will culture become effective to overcome destitution."[29] It is common knowledge that the expenditure in research and development is much higher in rich than in poor countries and that the concerns of the poorest people are barely taken into account, for instance, in medical research. This results in widening the cultural and technological gap between rich and poor people, not in promoting more equity.

Joseph Wresinski, who maintained a challenging dialog with academics for thirty years as the founder of the International Movement ATD Fourth World, drew from his experience as he articulated methods to effectively fight poverty and social exclusion. He stated that three different kinds of knowledge should be developed autonomously and that reciprocity should be established to cross-fertilize them (see Chapter 2). His starting questions were: what knowledge do the poorest people need, what knowledge do practitioners and action teams need, what knowledge do our national societies and our international communities need in order to effectively fight poverty and social exclusion?

The academic knowledge of poverty and social exclusion is necessary, yet it is but a partial fragmentary knowledge, indirect and purely informative, lacking the means to inspire and motivate people for action. A second type of knowledge, that of the poorest themselves, has to be developed and supported. The experience of our Movement suggests that it is the voice of the poorest that convinces citizens to take action, not its translation into academic studies. A third type of knowledge that needs to be recognized and supported, is that of men and women of action, who must remain autonomous to build this knowledge and free to pursue their own objectives.[30] Caught in the logic of a society that believes in the supremacy of academic knowledge, most research on poverty runs the danger of exploiting the poor and paralyzing their reasoning, because they take them as mere providers of information instead of individuals trying to understand and make sense of their situation. If there is something new to learn from people entrenched in poverty, it is

---

27. International Monetary Fund, *Review of the Poverty Reduction and Growth Facility: Issues and Options,* prepared by the Policy Development and Review and Fiscal Affairs Department, February 14, 2002, p. 6.

28. Michel Serres "Faire travailler la science à l'égalité", *revue Quart Monde,* 3ème trimestre 1991, Pages. 41to 43.

29. Michel Serres "Autour du père Joseph Wresinski", *revue Quart Monde,* septembre 1993, p. 8.

30. One might also acknowledge the existence of a fourth kind of knowledge through wisdom or spirituality, which is important to people who try to live up to a set of values and belong to communities of faith.

reciprocity, argues Joseph Wresinski. Moral and political responsibility as well as scientific rigour obliges universities and researchers to turn towards the poorest people to dialog with them and learn from them[31]:

> Scholars in the street, not to do research, not to stockpile information for themselves, but to let themselves be taught, be corrected, ready to call into question not only their knowledge, but the foundations, the methodology and the meaning of their knowledge....There is the true reversal, the only chance for a fundamental change in the assignment of roles.

Limits of an Academic Top-Down Approach

The building process of the WDR 2004 was that of an academic top-down approach, with its advantages and drawbacks. It was a helpful challenge taken up by the core writing team, to try to draw a worldwide picture of how services are working for poor people. The way they chose to perform the task was to draw heavily on existing research and to build an analytical framework making it possible to write a global synthesis. On the positive side, the report provides a lot of useful information and gives legitimacy to some fundamental claims on behavioral changes that are required. What is missing though is the participation of the poorest in the process itself.

Despite the real efforts of the core writing team which held consultations in around 20 countries, the knowledge building process of the report offered few opportunities to people entrenched in poverty and to those engaged with them to have their voice heard, because the academic format and the time constraints of the process did not make it possible. If they had been more closely associated with the work there is no doubt that the influence of tradition, of family links and of community belonging, on access to services—in short, the importance of culture—would have been better taken into account in the report.[32]

The one-year world consultation process through international meetings and through the Internet was mostly in English, in an economic language. Major western NGOs took part in the process with academics and civil servants. Only a small elite in developing countries was able and willing to participate. Moreover, due to the overly academic format of the report, very few books or papers from NGOs are quoted in its bibliography even when their ideas are taken over by the authors, which may give NGOs the feeling that their contribution is not really recognized and their knowledge is in some way "stolen," unlike the academic one.

There is a high risk that such a top-down approach might reinforce the power of the World Bank itself instead of empowering those who most need it: people mired in poverty and those who are committed with them in their fight against poverty. The authors try to avert that risk by insisting on the role poor people should play[33]:

> Governments and citizens can do better...by putting poor people at the center of service provision; by enabling them to monitor and discipline service providers; by amplifying their voice in policymaking; and by strengthening the incentives for providers to serve the poor.

---

31. Joseph Wresinski, *Defeating extreme poverty*, Lecture at the Sorbonne University, June 1, 1983. Available on www.atd-fourthworld.org.

32. As for access to education and health services, see for example the findings of 10 years work of a physician with very poor families in Madagascar; Dr. Chantal Laureau, "Les familles malgaches m'ont appris la santé," *revue Quart Monde* n° 184, November 2002, p. 42 to 45. See also Chapter 4 below.

33. WDR 2004, Overview, p. 1.

The authors write: "Emphasizing the power of clients is a welcome tone to the top-down technocratic orientation that has characterized much development thinking until now."[34]

The WDR 2004 itself can be considered a knowledge-based service, whose provider is the core writing team and whose first beneficiaries should be poor people through a very long route of accountability from Washington to the remotest places on earth. Therefore the authors' framework for analyzing service delivery and their findings can be applied to the very process they have implemented. Did they put poor people at the centre of their research process, enabling them to monitor their own work, amplifying their voice in policymaking? Did they put into practice their statement that "engaging poor clients in an active role as co-producers (the 'short route') can tremendously improve performance?"[35] It seems that researchers working on poverty were much more at the centre of the research process than the poor themselves. This gap between the stated principles and their implementation makes the report less convincing. Yet, if bridging this gap becomes a challenge to be taken up in the future, there is no limit to what we can hope for.

The Shortage of Truly Participatory Research on Poverty

In skimming through the awesome bibliography of the WDR 2004 one finds a shortage of research studies carried out in partnership with poor people.[36] Ethical issues of participatory approaches on poverty have been addressed and practical methods improved over the past decades.[37] Yet many research studies pretending to be "participatory" do not involve people with a background of poverty in all steps of research, from the definition of the goals and research topics to the revising of the final paper, but associate them at some late stage of the process, most often to extract some information from them. These research studies are more "extractive" than "participatory."

If participatory research too often fails people living in poverty and more so people living in extreme poverty, there are nevertheless strong examples that this can be effective. Over the years, ATD Fourth World has experienced this in informal and formal contexts. After years of community work in very poor areas, physicians wrote books about healthcare, merging the traditional knowledge of very poor families with their professional knowledge;[38] economists wrote books about work and unemployment with Fourth World delegates.[39] In more formal contexts, NGOs and researchers were asked by the federal Government in Belgium to write a general report on poverty, which they did with much input from people

---

34. WDR 2004 p. 65.

35. WDR 2004 p. 64.

36. See also for instance the contributions to the international conference "*Staying poor: chronic poverty and development policy*" on www.chronicpoverty.org/conference.htm

37. See for example the Chronic Poverty Research Center Toolbox, on http://idpm.man.ac.uk/cprc/CPToolbox

38. Docteur Isabelle Deligne et le club des bébés, *Grandir ensemble, parents et tout-petits*, Editions Quart Monde, Paris, 1993, 192 pages. Docteur Chantal Laureau et des familles de Tananarive, "Sarobidy ny silaky ny aina," Madagascar, 2000, 93 pages.

39. Xavier Godinot (under the direction of) *Finding work: tell us the secret! A dialogue on employment between unemployed workers, academic researchers, employers and policy-makers*, ATD Fourth World, 1995.

living in poverty over a two-year period.[40] This report had a major influence on subsequent Belgian anti-poverty policies. The methodology for the merging of different types of knowledge, putting together high-level academics, practitioners and people living in extreme poverty as co-researchers and co-writers, was investigated and rigorously experimented and assessed.[41] The methodology of common training, bringing together practitioners from different disciplines (teachers, nurses, lawyers, policemen, and so forth) with people living in poverty, has been rigorously experimented and is beginning to spread.[42]

Why are participatory approaches so rare? The WDR 2004 comes up with the right explanation: "Even if we know what has to be done, it may be difficult to get it done, despite the urgent need of the world's poor people," because "many of the changes involve fundamental shifts in power—something that cannot happen overnight."[43] Real participatory research requires a power sharing between researchers and people living in poverty, not at the expense of scientific rigour, which is strengthened, but at the expense of unwillingness to cross social barriers. If more freedom and empowerment is to be gained by people living in extreme poverty over their own lives through the "demand driven assistance" put forward by this report, an attitude of responsiveness, solidarity and humility is needed from the powerful, whether it be rich countries, multinational institutions, researchers, national or local leaders, or second line and front line providers. From his indepth investigation of Wresinski's approach, Christopher Winship, professor of sociology at Harvard University, concludes: "It is only by fundamentally changing our relationship to the poor that true change will be possible."[44]

Conclusion

"Poverty in an age of affluence is being unable to write and having others write about you."[45] Eradicating extreme poverty demands learning from the poorest themselves about what poverty is and building up with them a more comprehensive knowledge of how things happen and what needs to be done. There is no doubt that the World Bank could do a lot to support more participatory approaches to poverty and help generate a more comprehensive and effective knowledge that would include that of the very poor themselves. "Putting poor people at the center of service provision; enabling them to monitor and discipline service providers; amplifying their voice in policymaking," all these claims of the WDR 2004 are utterly justified. It must be stressed that they are also very demanding for all actors including the World Bank itself.

---

40. *Rapport Général sur la Pauvreté en Belgique*, Union des Villes et des Communes de Belgique, Fondation Roi Baudoin, ATD Quart Monde, 1995, 424 pages.

41. Groupe de Recherche Quart Monde-Université, *Le croisement des savoirs. Quand le Quart Monde et l'Université pensent ensemble*, éditions de l'Atelier et éditions Quart Monde, 1999, 525 pages.

42. ATD Fourth World UK, *Talk with us, not at us*, 1996 ; Groupe de recherche action-formation Quart Monde Partenaire, *Le croisement des pratiques. Quand le Quart Monde et les professionnels se forment ensemble*, éditions Quart Monde, mars 2002, 227 pages.

43. WDR 2004, Overview, p. 18.

44. Christopher Winship, preface to the English edition of *The poor are the church, A conversation with Fr. Joseph Wresinski* by Gilles Anouilh, Twenty-Third publications, 2002, p. xii.

45. Words from postcard, quoted by Anne Corden, *Writing about poverty: ethical dilemmas*, Hartley Dean editor, Ethics and Social Policy Research, University of Luton Press/Social Policy Association, 1996.

PART II

Experiences from Developing Countries

Making Health Services Work for Poor People: Ten Years of Work in Tananarive, Madagascar

Chantal Laureau, Caroline Blanchard, and Xavier Godinot[46]

The setting for this chapter is a Tananarive neighborhood with around six thousand inhabitants. Precarious and densely populated dwellings, a few drinking fountains, no toilets, and flooding during the rainy season render hygiene almost non-existent. The parents have unstable jobs in the informal economy and with a surprising amount of inventiveness and energy try to provide their children with an education. In 1991, ATD Fourth World, together with parents, launched a dual program to promote health care (which went on to last for ten years) and knowledge sharing (which is ongoing). At the beginning, relations between the inhabitants and the health care services were shaped by a lack of understanding and fear, with inhabitants resorting to the ancestral knowledge of traditional medicine and health care staff reacting mostly according to the norms of Western medicine. After several years of work allowing the parents' capabilities to be appreciated and strengthened, dialog was made possible. This meant that new paths could be opened based on greater understanding and mutual respect.

Living Conditions and Health Care Provision in Tananarive

The program was developed in a part of the Antohomadinika neighborhood, located in the first suburb of Antananarivo (Tananarive), a city of around one million inhabitants and the capital of Madagascar. The ATD Fourth World Movement settled in this suburb in 1991.

---

46. The three authors are permanent volunteers in the International ATD Fourth World Movement. Chantal Laureau has worked for ten years as a physician in Tananarive. Caroline Blanchard and Xavier Godinot work at the Research and Training Institute close to Paris. We thank Daniel Fayard and Aude Magnier for editing the French version of this paper.

At this time, it was a very poor neighborhood without a state school or a church,[47] though parish representatives live there. Chantal Laureau, the first permanent ATD Fourth World volunteer sent to Madagascar, had created links with this neighborhood's inhabitants as of 1989 while working as a doctor with the Missionaries of Charity Brothers.[48] She received office visits twice a week on the Brothers' premises and this let Chantal Laureau come into contact with families from the neighborhood and appreciate the inhabitants' level of health. She also met a neighborhood inhabitant who later introduced her to several families. The reception given by the local council representative (Fokontany) and contact with the Antohomadinika catholic parish church provided further access to the neighborhood. It was later chosen due, on the one hand, to its level of poverty and isolation, and on the other to the relations built over two years.

Antohomadinika is a sprawling neighborhood to the west of Antananarivo, mostly built on old paddy fields that have been drained, to a greater or lesser extent. "Antohomadinika" means "the place where there are small fish" as you can fish in the old paddy fields during the rainy season. This agricultural area attracted a large number of people and was developed at the beginning of the 20th century when a nearby railway station was built. The neighborhood is split into five Fokontany[49] (administrative units), which are also subdivided into sectors. The residents of each sector elect a coordination committee, whose chairman is the only person to be paid. This committee manages everything to do with hygiene, security, collective contributions for funerals, and relations with the state school. Initial administrative steps are taken at the Fokontany office, where a secretary works, paid through contributions made by inhabitants. The inhabitants must attend the meetings in the Fokontany and their presence is recorded in a register. It is also a place of mediation where people try to resolve neighborhood disputes before resorting to the police or a judge.

ATD Fourth World is present in the five sectors of Fokontany "III G Hangar," which is a subneighborhood with around 6,000 inhabitants of which 1,800 are children aged between 0 and 15.[50] It comprises a maze of tiny streets inaccessible by car and a succession of intertwining rooms, invisible from the main road and next to a railway line that is no longer in service. Along one side runs a very busy street where there are two taxi-brousse stops, a small market, small businesses, restaurants and spice shops. The streets are very crowded and there are a lot of hawkers and tiny spice stalls.

The inhabitants of this Fokontany are relatively heterogeneous. There are families living in the most extreme poverty but also people belonging to the middle class (primary school teachers, civil servants). A lot of families are still very much in touch with their rural origins; sometimes they have land or a house in the country. After a few years, most of the families settle in the city for good and take in their parents in unplanned constructions that sprawl further and further. More often than not, people live in a shed made out of planks of wood and a steel sheet roof, often flattened 200-liter drums. The floor is of beaten earth, on top

---

47. There is a state school open to this neighborhood's inhabitants, but the children rarely attend it.

48. Established in Tananarive for several years prior to Chantal Laureau's arrival, they had set up small schools and built a dispensary, where they attended to their pupils' family members.

49. Antsalovana, Antohomadinika South, FTA, IVO, Antohomadinika avaratra, and Antohomadinika III G Hangar. The work of ATD Fourth World focuses on Antohomadinika III G Hangar. In 2004, the administrative authorities reorganised the city into only four Fokontany.

50. Estimates from the team of volunteers' survey carried out in the neighborhood in 1996.

of which a straw mat has been placed. Many inhabitants have neither electricity nor running water or only one of the two. Having water is an ongoing concern. There is a long wait at the washing station and the drinking fountains (three in 1991, five in 2000), which are closed at night. The lack of toilets is a major problem: the adults must go to public toilets over a kilometer away or wait until nighttime to go to the old paddy fields. People have to pay to use the public toilets recently funded by Care International, which have hardly changed the situation. The fact that there are no garbage containers also testifies to the terrible health conditions in which people live.

The lack of space forces people to be always outside. However, during the rainy season, the small yards at the back of the houses become muddy and unusable. Even during the dry season, as the water table is only ten centimeters under the ground, the rooms are damp and can be flooded. All of Antananarivo's low-level neighborhoods, which were built on former paddy fields, can become flooded when it rains.

The majority of the inhabitants in this Fokontany do not have a set income. They often work in the informal economy and live from one day to the next, together with the lack of security which such an existence brings with it. Very few have work contracts. The men sell salvage goods or food, go to building sites and wait until they are taken on, unload trucks at the market, or pull carts. The women take care of all of the household duties. To complement the family's earnings, they wash clothes, deliver water, work as sales people (for example, selling food that they themselves have prepared), seamstresses, and maids. Some women work in the factories in the free zone.

There is a strong spiritual expression in the neighborhood and religion is prevalent. The inhabitants are either catholic, protestant, or adherents of a more hidden traditional religion. Nearly every day, groups of "preachers" pass through the neighborhood to sing, pray outdoors, or preach to the crowd. Many of the neighborhood's very poor families attend evangelical churches.

There are public and private dispensaries and hospitals near the neighborhood that are rarely visited by Antohomadinika inhabitants. The two public dispensaries are situated in Ambodin'Isotry and Antanimena, ten minutes and 20 minutes away on foot, respectively. The two private dispensaries, the Missionaries of Charity Brothers' dispensary and a Lutheran clinic, are 15 minutes walk away. Tsaralalana children's hospital in the city center is easy to get to as are the two university hospitals, one specializing in medicine and the other in surgery. Several private doctors have set up their consultancies nearby.

In 1991, the health situation was very worrying. Infant mortality was very high and life expectancy very short. There are no reliable statistics for this area as most of the children are not registered at birth and do not have a "kopia" (birth certificate). Only doctors and midwives have the authority to grant a birth certificate, which is required by the state registrar, despite the fact that legally a witness is sufficient. Women who do not give birth at the hospital or use the services of a doctor or midwife cannot have their child registered. This later poses an obstacle to the child's schooling. In June 2005, UNICEF estimated that there were around 2.5 million unregistered children in Madagascar out of an estimated population of 17 million.[51]

---

51. UNICEF source (http://www.unicef.org/infobycountry/madagascar_27369.html).

The Decision to Carry Out an Early Childhood Program (1989–1990)

From the first few months spent in the Madagascan capital, the ATD Fourth World Movement's permanent volunteers were aware of the very fragile health of young children and the impressive efforts by the inhabitants of Antohomadinika for their development given the scarcity of the means available to them. The mortality rate of young children is very high, and they sometimes die of benign illnesses that could have been cured quite cheaply. There are many poorly nourished children. None of the children that Chantal Laureau sees in consultation has a normal growth curve. Many mothers have lost one or more children through malnutrition, which is exacerbated by births occurring at close intervals. The majority of mothers taking part in the early childhood program have lost a child.

A lot of children are called Solo, which means "replacement," a name traditionally given to a child who is born after the death of an older sibling. Nevertheless, the effort made by the inhabitants to make up for all that is lacking must also be brought to light. The poorly nourished children smile a lot. This shows that those around them stimulate the children enough to counter the behavioral problems inflicted by the illness. In general, the whole family shows a lot of affection towards the children, who receive a lot of attention but who also become independent from an early age. From the age of two or three, the children can make up games, play alone for hours on end and help their parents by doing some shopping. In view of the relatively confined and dangerous surroundings in which they live, the children cope surprisingly well and have few accidents. The parents go to considerable lengths to have them cured. Consequently, the need for an early childhood program grew gradually. The dual aim was to respond to the distress felt by the parents in view of all of those children who were dying and to highlight and strengthen the parents' knowledge.

Box 4.1: Infant and Child Mortality in Madagascar

According to UNICEF, the mortality rate of children aged under five in Madagascar was 186 per 1,000 children in 1960 and 126 per 1,000 children in 2003. Infant mortality (from 0 to 1 year) was 112 per 1,000 in 1960 and 78 per 1,000 in 2003. Life expectancy at the time of birth was 54 years in 2003. Between 1998 and 2003, 14 percent of babies suffered from hypotrophy (insufficient weight); 49 percent of children aged under five suffered from stunted growth between 1995 and 2003.[52]

From the outset, this program closely combined the two dimensions of health promotion and knowledge sharing in the spirit of the ATD Fourth World founder[53]:

> To know is first to be conscious of being a person. It is to give a meaning to what one lives and be able to express it. It is…to know one's roots, to identify with a family, with a community. To know is to be capable of understanding one's experience and of sharing them with others.

---

52. UNICEF source (http://www.unicef.org/infobycountry/madagascar_statistics.html#10).

53. Joseph Wresinski, Fourth World Review n° 105–106, *The Fourth World child in search of knowledge,* 2nd quarter 1979, p. 7.

The least favored, he adds later, have knowledge and culture, "but this knowledge and culture are truncated" and do not give them a place in the world.[54]

> The knowledge and thoughts of the very poor are all the more fragile because those whose ideas can neither be expressed nor heard cannot firmly state their own beliefs. That is why they are also the playthings of all arbitrary authorities.

Enabling them to access "knowledge" as defined previously is a vital step in their empowerment. This makes it indispensable to give a strong cultural dimension to every project designed for their development. Never tiring of listening to the least favored, encouraging them to express themselves as individuals and as a group, and letting them gain a sense of their own worth and the fundamentals to converse with people from other backgrounds—these are the marks of the work to empower the inhabitants carried out by the ATD Fourth World team.

Starting Point: Lack of Understanding and a Divide Between the Hospitals and the Inhabitants

Over the years, by immersing itself in the neighborhood, the ATD Fourth World team discovered the depth of the chasm separating Antohomadinika inhabitants from the medical services that are supposed to be there to help.

Madagascan doctors are trained according to Western methods, based on looking for signs to support a diagnosis affecting an organ. The person's background, relationships, and environment are rarely taken into consideration. This approach, which prevails worldwide, creates a certain disdain towards traditional healing. However, the inhabitants of Antohomadinika have a traditional approach towards events according to a set of beliefs that give a meaning to each gesture. These different views of illness together with a mutual lack of understanding partly explain the fear felt by the inhabitants towards the medical world and sometimes the humiliating reactions of competent doctors. The parents are attentive towards their children but this is not immediately apparent to the medical staff. For example, mothers traditionally are afraid that the newborn will get a cold stomach and prefer not to undress the baby. This obviously goes against the rules of hygiene that stress the importance of bathing newborns. These differing views of a situation contribute to creating cultural barriers that render dialog impossible. Individuals trained in a traditional approach quite simply do not have any say in the explanations given by a medical staff member trained according to Western methods.

In a society in which it is essential not to be alone but in a group when there is a birth, illness, or death, a hospital is seen as a cold, fearful place that is only used as a last resort. It is often associated with death and humiliation. Doctors do not understand why their advice is not followed while parents prefer to cure their child according to traditional methods and remedies which mean something to them. Fed up with being constantly thwarted by people whose illnesses could have been cured if they had come earlier, the medical staff becomes aggressive towards the parents who, they believe, are irresponsible. The staff concludes

---

54. Joseph Wresinski, *Culture and Extreme Poverty*, conference speech given in 1985, Cahiers Wresinski n° 7, Fourth World editions, 2004, p. 25.

that the parents do not love their children as they do not administer the treatment pre-scribed or they wait until the child is in agony before bringing him to the hospital. There is a total lack of understanding, as is shown by the attitude of the mother who refused to come to the Mother and Child Protection clinic and traveled for miles to take her poorly nourished child to a healer.

Madagascan traditional medicine is full of enormous possibilities and alleviates certain illnesses very well. "Tambavy," plant infusions, can be highly effective but also very dan-gerous if they are used incorrectly. Matrons, who live in the same neighborhood and often in the same conditions as very poor people, hold a privileged position in the administer-ing of this medicine. They are therefore the close and preferred contact that accompanies the mother before the birth. They recommend prenatal visits that are held in their own homes. They know and give massages that are often effective: when necessary, they can change the baby's position inside the womb. They play an important role before and dur-ing the birth and in the first few months of the baby's life. In the neighborhood, the sick willingly use traditional remedies which they know and understand and which respect their beliefs and traditions. Most Madagascans use "tambavy." Only those who suffer from nega-tive side effects are hospitalized. Since the doctors see only these people, and therefore, only the downside of these remedies, they advise people not to use them at all. Consequently, those who are hospitalized do not dare say that they have used tambavy. Mutual distrust is hence built on a combination of misunderstandings and ignorance.

For Antohomadinika inhabitants, a hospital is a place in which they are stigmatized and seen as poor and different. They do not always have time to change or wash their clothes before coming, especially in an emergency, and are quickly labeled and criticized by the medical staff due to their appearance. Furthermore, the hospital fees constitute an additional barrier for those who are very poor. Substantial payment is sometimes needed in hospitals in Madagascar. The patient must bring his own sheet or blanket. What can be done when there is only one blanket for the whole family? Because of unfamiliarity, lack of understanding, and humilia-tion, the inhabitants were very fearful of the hospital. Although most medical personnel in Madagascar work in very difficult conditions and are poorly paid, some among them were open-minded and made sure, for example, that there was medicine set aside for poor families.

Implementation of the Knowledge-Health Program Around Those in Early Childhood

The knowledge-health program began through continuing ATD Fourth World coopera-tion with the Missionaries of Charity Brothers. Chantal Laureau complemented the medical visits on the Brothers' premises with a nutritional followup that started in January 1991. Mothers who were seen in a checkup were invited, when necessary, to a second longer checkup to organize a nutritional followup to talk about the food given to their children. A monthly "dish demonstration" complemented the nutritional followup. The ATD Fourth World team[55] suggested to mothers whose children had symptoms of malnutrition that they learn how to make a simple and cheap dish that provides all of the necessary nutrients.

---

55. This team was then strengthened through the presence of new foreign volunteers and by Madagascan friends who contributed with their own knowledge and their translation skills.

Home visits were organized with the aim of seeing children who came to a checkup, especially very undernourished children who are very fragile and fall sick easily. The mothers showed how much these visits meant to them: *"Nobody had ever come to our home, except for you."* These visits gave rise to relationships of trust and created a certain dynamic: the ATD Fourth World volunteers were awaited and the inhabitants cleaned their homes to welcome them. During these home visits, development activities were often suggested for the very young children. The visit then became a time in which the family enjoyed itself around books. The young children were the center of attention and the other family members played an active part.

The link between knowledge and health was a key part of this program. While the "street libraries" were organized for children aged between five and twelve (book based entertainment in the street to show children the pleasures of knowledge, art and beauty), a health program for the women was held nearby.

This program developed by trial and error through discussions with the mothers and attempts to meet their aspirations in various ways. For a long time the Fourth World volunteers did not know why the children were so undernourished. Their understanding grew progressively through action. While trust started to blossom, the parents expressed themselves more and shed light on this question. For example, they are convinced of the fundamental importance of rice, a staple food in Madagascan cooking. Their proverbs state that a child is well if he eats rice. Conversely, if he does not eat rice, even if he eats well and enough, the parents worry. Their nutritional references are different. All of this only becomes apparent with time, and as long as there is a strong personal commitment trust is built. So as to complement the volunteers' knowledge and understanding of the country, they were posted in other places. Chantal Laureau went along with a doctor visiting the patients in a pediatrics clinic, another permanent volunteer worked in a nursery school, and another in a home for children placed by the justice department.

In 1992, informal meetings with women from the neighborhood began to let them ask questions they had about their health and that of their children and to give them some fundamental facts to confront malnutrition. They were also about valuing all that the neighborhood's inhabitants do to contribute to their child's personal development. Indeed, the parents prove to be highly inventive in their children's development considering the lack of means at their disposal. For example, a mother told us that she cut out pictures from magazines and covered the walls of her home with them to teach her daughter the names of the objects. Another aim of these meetings is to encourage the women to talk to each other, exchange advice and experience and strengthen their solidarity. The team had indeed noticed a certain distrust within the neighborhood that was particularly heightened by the fear of poisoning, which people spoke about a great deal. At first these meetings took place once a month and always in the same place. By the end of 1993 meetings with the mothers were held weekly in different places and were complemented with activities for the children. Relations in the neighborhood improved to a certain extent as a result. One mother said: "We are happy; we have hope for our children's future. If we are sick, there is someone to cure us." Another positive sign was the ongoing presence of the mothers at the nutritional checkups arranged for their children.

In 1993, thanks to the work of neighborhood leaders and the support of the Sentinelles NGO, a dispensary was opened in a sector of Fokontany III G Hangar and another was opened in Tsaramasay where Chantal Laureau would later run a Mother and Child Protection consultation until 1999.

Extending the Knowledge-Health Program

From June 1992 to July 1994, the ATD Fourth World team consisted of an average of three core workers supported by other volunteers. It was expanded in August 1994 with an average of five core workers, two of which were Madagascan nationals as of 1998–99. In 1995, the team decides to expand its field of action in favor of health by incorporating this subject into all of its cultural activities. Work is stepped up with more regular visits, particularly in two small courtyards. These moments of leisure between the mother and her young children are complemented by a systematic visit to the homes of the mothers who take part. The sessions in the small courtyards are organized accordingly. Everyone is invited to wash his hands, a time in which news is exchanged and possibly volunteers are invited to visit a sick person at home. Then a coordinator tells a story. In the same place and in a small area, two activities are held: the street library, on the one hand, and the health program, on the other. After the story, simple educational and development games are presented to the mothers, who are invited to play with their last-born present for the rest of the session. The mothers are fully involved in the activity, making them their child's first teacher. They feel at greater ease to ask questions when they see themselves in this role. In a very informal way, discussions allow the women to gradually learn more about their body, the nutritional value of food, family planning. In 1995, this activity reached 57 children in one courtyard, of which there were around 20 regular participants, and 47 children in the other courtyard, of which 15 were regular participants.

Over the following years, the cultural work undertaken by the ATD Fourth World team took on a new scope. The team had noticed the overwhelming appeal that books had on the neighborhood's children and, soon after, their parents. One day in October 1997, some mothers spoke with the street library coordinators and asked to be lent books that they could read at home, so as to learn and tell the stories to their children. Soon after, nine parents started to be lent books. Four years later, there were 340 youngsters and adults registered for this service, which the coordination team could no longer fulfill. After a meeting with the chairman and vice-chairman of the Fokontany, it was decided to build a library on land that had just been given to the neighborhood.[56] The library was built in 2003 by some ten adults from the neighborhood who were hired for this task.

The Development Books

To complement the knowledge-health activities in the small courtyards, the team organized the systematic followup of children born in 1995 and the beginning of 1996. Mothers were invited to fill in their child's development book. Here they wrote about the birth and the key moments at the start of the child's life as well as his progress. Some mothers also mentioned the hopes they had for the child; "I would like you to learn to read and write, and to talk how we should talk." Others explained their view of education: "The aim of parents is to see their children succeed in life [...]"; "We encourage you so that you learn manners

---

56. François Philiponeau, *The pride of a Madagascan neighborhood* Journal Feuille de Route, April 2003, p 3.

and know how to write [...]"; "When he does something naughty, we give him a good telling off." In 1997, 26 women, accompanied by the ATD Fourth World team, decided to fill in a development book for their child. The writing of these books meant that discussions with the mothers on their practices could be deepened. In the life of the least favored families, health often comes after family unity. A breastfeeding mother cannot be hospitalized without risking the death of her child, who would not bear to be torn away so harshly. Family unity sometimes comes before hospitalizing one of its members. "Parents often prefer keeping the family together to healing a child. In any case, the child may not be cured and if he is it won't last if the family goes through particularly hard times."[57] "Health is the balance between a person, his environment and the community in which he lives. Illness upsets this balance."[58] Health also relies on solidarity. Hospitalization is only possible if there is solidarity around the sick person with some people agreeing to look after the children and others offering financial support. Efforts to improve hygiene in the neighborhood require a change of attitude by everybody.

Dialog with Health Professionals and Medical Bodies

The lack of understanding between the medical staff and the neighborhood's parents as well as the fear that results in parents putting off a visit to the hospital for as long as possible are still tangible problems. As trust had been firmly established with the parents, who have gotten used to meeting to speak about health and share the way they do things, in 1997 the ATD Fourth World team decided to organize an exchange with the health professionals. Mothers were invited to visit health care centers around Antohomadinika to meet the staff and better understand the care on offer. They hence discovered the Isotry dispensary, Tsaralalana children's hospital, the Marie Stopes International dispensary.

Health professionals were also invited to meetings with the neighborhood mothers. A group of health care professionals, mostly from Befelatanana hospital, was formed at the end of 1996 to analyze what they knew about the families' experiences. When they learn

---

Box 4.2: Dialog Between the Very Poor and Health Services

In 1997, during a meeting between a doctor, a nurse, and neighborhood inhabitants, people started to talk about the mutual lack of understanding that existed. At the end of the meeting, a mother asked: "Can a child die if he has a needle in his head." She had finally managed to ask this question two years after her baby's death. Her daughter had had a cranial perfusion, which is always shocking. She had never been able to speak about it. Her question fully embodied the incapacity, fear and shame of very poor people to talk with "those who know," the suffering of ignorance which people dare not mention and also the inability of the professionals to see this gap and bridge it.

---

57. Laureau Chantal, "*Madagascan families taught me about health*" in *Fourth World*, n°184, November 2002.
58. *Ibid.*

Box 4.3: A Nurse's Experience

Janine, a pediatric nurse, did not understand why the children were brought to the hospital so late. She thought that the parents did not look after them well. In 1996, the ATD Fourth World team invited her to a meeting on health with some mothers in the neighborhood of Antohoma-dinika. During this meeting, the mothers explained to her all the steps they take when a child is sick: the use of traditional medicine, the never-ending search for money by offering to wash laundry or deliver water, the purchase at the market of medicine whose name they have remembered, a visit to the doctor, the attempts to improve the child's nutrition, and so forth. They mentioned their questions and uncertainties with regard to the hospital and the fear of only finding a lack of understanding there.

Janine was overwhelmed: before her were women she thought she knew well as she often saw them at the hospital. At the hospital they were ashamed and incapable of answering her questions nor did they dare tell her the truth. Here she saw them as responsible, inventive, and brave. Understanding was born: Janine agreed to learn from these women and let them teach her. Trust started to grow on both sides. She gradually committed herself to the people in the neighborhood, with whom she now has a very close relationship. Moms who have to go to the hospital feel more confident. "Go on," they say to each other, "there's Janine in the pediatrics department. She's nice, she doesn't shout." Having friendly relations with a nurse from the hospital is reassuring and makes the mothers in the neighborhood proud.

---

about the people's living conditions, the professionals can appreciate the effort required to go to a hospital. Children must be looked after. The time spent getting to and staying at the hospital is time not worked. Even going to the hospital can be expensive. Highly precarious living conditions also represent a barrier to following a specific treatment. The mothers dared to talk unashamedly about resorting to traditional methods, something they would never do inside a hospital.

During these meetings, the professionals, who come to meet families where they live, discover women, whom they only see frightened and ashamed in the hospital, in a different light. This can lead to relations being started afresh, as is shown by a nurse's account of her experience.

Writing a Book on the Health of Very Young Children

At this time, there were few books written in Madagascan and practically none on early childhood. The idea therefore arose to produce a book that would provide answers to the questions most often asked by parents. The book would also show the inventiveness of parents when confronted by the multiple challenges posed by a child's education. This book would also be a means to pursue discussions with the health care professionals. It gradually started to take shape as of 1995 and was published in May 2000 under the title *Sarobidy Ny Silaky Ny Aina* which means "Our children are a treasure." A simple collection of words from the parents to start with, it was later complemented with information contained in the children's development books and then reorganized by subject in cooperation with the health care professionals. They helped by rereading the work, correcting what they considered to be wrong and highlighting what seemed important in the development and health of a young Madagascan child. This work contributed to creating a common language between two worlds whose relations are often strained. It illustrated how knowledge really can be shared between people from a very poor background and health care professionals.

Today, the neighborhood's inhabitants are very proud of the book, which is a starting point for conversation in the neighborhood and with institutions.

> This book aims to be an invitation for health care professionals to dare meet very poor families […] The book says that such a meeting is possible and that everyone comes out on top if we heed the concerns of others: if both professionals and parents look for a better future for their children together, parents could learn from the professionals and the professionals, having learned why the parents are afraid, could cure their children better.[59]

Funding granted by the World Bank through the Health Ministry allowed 200 more copies of the book to be published in 2002. By showing how much the parents love their children, think about their education, and exert energy for them, this book helped to change the reputation of a neighborhood that is all too often talked about in negative terms.

People and a Neighborhood Gaining Freedom and Pride

We chose to focus on health, but our work had a wider effect on the neighborhood. Other meetings were arranged around books and sport, delegates took part in international meetings abroad, talks were held between Antohomadinika inhabitants and those from another poor neighborhood on the island of La Réunion. A whole team was mobilized and together thought about apparently unresolvable situations, taking time to write about what they learned from the people they had met so as to interiorize their life and better understand them. The inhabitants of Antohomadinika were therefore met in a wider context than just as part of a program on the mortality of young children, whose effects are clearly not restricted to health. During a checkup, a mother said, "Since I have been taking part in the meetings during which we talk about health, I have dared visit my son's primary school teacher who was unfair to him." The effect of the knowledge-health program cannot therefore only be measured according to health and medical criteria.

On October 17, 2003, the World Day to Overcome Extreme Poverty, national authorities inaugurated the permanent library "Fanovozantsoa Joseph Wresinski" in Fokontany III G Hangar after ten years of activities run by the street library. The inhabitants were overjoyed and said, "Now they'll no longer say we're a shantytown but: 'Antohomadinika, the place where there's a library.'" The book written with the parents has an important place there, and the librarians are mothers from the neighborhood who have received training at the municipal library. The fact that several hundred people attended the inauguration together with the local and national authorities shows the importance of this event for the neighborhood, whose reputation has changed thanks to these different projects.[60] At the time ATD Fourth World set itself up in the neighborhood, there were no other associations present. In 2000, several associations appeared and their number is still growing: Inter Aide, Sentinelles, Terre des Hommes, Care International. During a vaccination campaign, a doctor from Inter

---

59. *Sorobidy Ny Silaky Ny Aina*, extract from the introduction by Chantal Laureau.
60. François Philiponeau, *Books open your mind*, Journal Feuille de Route, November–December 2003, p. 3.

Box 4.4: Leaving Fear Behind: The Account in 2004 of the Path Traveled by One Mother

---

"Before, when the children were sick, I always took them to a doctor. One day, my nine-month old daughter was very sick. I took her to a doctor although I didn't have any money. I borrowed some money off the neighbors. The doctor gave us a paper to hospitalize my daughter but I hid the paper and went to see another doctor. I saw seven doctors, all of them wanted to hospitalize her. She was getting more and more sick and I was very scared of going to the hospital. For me, it was the last resort. Seeing that my daughter was very sick, I decided to go to the nearest hospital. A few meters before the entrance to the hospital, the child died. My husband and I did not go home but took a bus to bury her at the family vault. We only have very little money and my husband told me not to cry or the bus driver would realize that the child was dead. We would have had to pay a great deal...I did not cry, I only trembled...I lowered my head so people could not see my face. When I found my family, I fainted...It is hard being a slave to fear. Later on I came across the ATD Fourth World Movement, which helped me to fight my fear. With volunteers, we have visited hospitals, met people in hospital and found out about the procedure to be hospitalized. It helped me a lot. Since then, I have helped others who are scared of going to hospital. It is not only the fear of the hospital that the Movement helped me get over but also the fear to change my views. With the Movement, I have fought really hard for my right to health care. Having access to health care formed part of my rights and now I am no longer afraid of hospitals. I have not kept this just for me but I try to help others who are still prisoners of this fear."

Aide said that it was easier to mobilize the people from this neighborhood than from others as they were more open-minded. The work undertaken over ten years clearly played a part in achieving such open-mindedness. The accounts of the mothers, some of which are shown in boxes, also reveal the path they have traveled and the commitment they are capable of taking to help others progress. An important factor to bear in mind in the assessment is the strengthening of local solidarity. Some women say, "We didn't dare before but now we visit each other to share advice."

Box 4.5: A Mother's Account, End of 2004

"...Good health is the most precious possession. In my neighborhood there was a child who was seriously sick. He had a swollen belly because he had not been to the toilet in several days. The child's parents did not want to go to the hospital. They went to various soothsayers and traditional healers. All of the healers said that the child was possessed. I advised them to go to the hospital but they turned my suggestion down as the healers had forbidden them from going there. Afterwards, the mom said that she didn't know the hospital. So I picked up the child and took him to the hospital. I don't know if I did the right thing or caused a commotion. After the checkup, the doctor had him hospitalized straight away due to the seriousness of the child's illness. The parents could not watch over their child at the hospital as they were too frightened (you need an attendant for someone to be hospitalized) and they looked for a way to sneak the child out of the hospital. My husband and I slept on the hospital's cement floor and did not take our eyes off him as we were worried that the parents would come and fetch him. After a few days, they learnt that the child's health had improved and they thanked us dearly. They also heard the doctor say, "If you had waited another day, the child could have died." The parents were happy to discover that we do not need to be clever or have qualifications to go to the hospital. They also learnt that going to the hospital is beneficial to the person who is sick."

Some Lessons Learned from the Program

This brief account spanning just over ten years of work provides important information on how to make health services work for poor people by outlining a long-term approach with a bottom-up focus.

"Freedom from illness and freedom from illiteracy—two of the most important ways in which poor people can escape poverty—remain elusive to many," states the 2004 World Bank report on World Development. This report reads,

> The fact that there are strong examples where services do work means governments and citizens can do better. How? By putting poor people at the center of service provision: by enabling them to monitor and discipline service providers, by amplifying their voice in policymaking, and by strengthening the incentives for providers to serve the poor.

Faced with the actual situation experienced by the poor in Antohomadinika, these aims appear so distant that they are out of reach. Very often, the wealthy echelons, such as institutions, protect themselves against the very poor, who are seen as a threat to their safety, health, and reputation. In all of the main cities throughout the world, the wealthy form ghettos to protect themselves from the poor with walls and sometimes guards. Who is going to "put poor people at the center of service provision" while such services are designed to keep them out? How are shantytown moms, most of whom are scared stiff of a hospital, going to "discipline service providers" and "monitor service provision"? The poorest people are dominated by others in the political, economic, social and cultural fields. They are excluded from the decision-making bodies where their fate is decided. How can they be given more control over their own lives and more influence on the institutions that should be open to them? What does the account on the ten years of work in Antohomadinika teach us?

From a Dead End to a Partnership

The theoretical contributions of the book "Artisans of Democracy"[61] provide an initial interpretation of this account. On the basis of 12 case studies, this book seeks to understand how citizens can re-establish the connection between institutions, which should be available to all, and the poorest people who do not benefit from such institutions. It identifies processes and stages to this approach.

The start of the account is marked by the alarming health situation in the neighborhood of Antohomadinika: perinatal and infant mortality is extremely high and the healthcare infrastructure appears inefficient and incapable of providing the inhabitants with greater well-being. There is a total lack of understanding between medical staff and the neighborhood's inhabitants: it is a dead end. Both parties are stuck in a situation of failure and a lack of understanding that is going nowhere and where relations are non-existent. The inhabitants have accepted this dead end and expect almost nothing from the hospital, which gives its staff the

61. Jona M. Rosenfeld & Bruno Tardieu, *Artisans of Democracy. How ordinary people, families in extreme poverty and social institutions become allies to overcome social exclusion*, University Press of America, 2000.

opportunity to say that they are not valid partners. There may be people within the hospital who sympathize with the inhabitants' situation but feel powerless to change the institution.

At the end of the account, a partnership starts to bud between the neighborhood's inhabitants and the medical staff. Both parties have learnt to get to know and respect each other more, the inhabitants dare to go to the hospital more often when they need to. Everyone, the institution and the inhabitants, finds it useful to invest time in a relationship which now appears fruitful. Both parties have changed. Accordingly, the medical services start to have a real positive impact on the health of the neighborhood's inhabitants. The impact at the end of the account clashes with the impasse at the beginning. The nuances of such a relative success must be told as the inhabitants' living conditions remain excessively precarious and perinatal and infant death very high.[62] Nevertheless, there have been changes that make the two parties feel proud and this constitutes a measure of success. What stages brought about such an achievement?

Putting the Poor at the Center, A Lifelong Commitment

The 2004 World Bank report on World Development rightly states that for services to work well for the poorest these people must be "put at the center of service provision." But what does this mean? Putting poor people, who are both dominated and excluded, at the center of service provision involves, on the one hand, considerably empowering poor people's capacities and, on the other, changing the attitude of those who are not poor, which is no less of a feat. This sometimes translates into a "U-turn" in favor of the poor. In the account in question, how were the least favored "empowered" and how was the "U-turn" of those who contributed to excluding the poor brought about?

At the origin of the program there was the arrival in Madagascar of a permanent ATD Fourth World volunteer who had taken the decision to place the poorest people at the center of her life. Most of the four hundred permanent ATD Fourth World volunteers carry with them the faces of children, youngsters and adults scarred by poverty who transformed their view of the world and of their own life. They have committed themselves to this Movement because they reject the unacceptable situation of ongoing poverty and exclusion. Following on from the founder of the Movement, Joseph Wresinski, they voluntarily chose to

> give the least favored minorities priority in all regards. Their interests will come first and will be the best attended.…Bringers of change in any society, they will be the experts in our projects of a new civilization and their advance will be the measure of our own progress

as stated in the Basic Beliefs of this Movement adopted in 1965. These Basic Beliefs indicate an approach to follow that each person strives to put into practice to the best of his own ability. All ATD Fourth World volunteers accept a simple way of life and a very modest income that does not reflect their qualifications or length of service, so that they can remain close to the poorest people.

---

62. UNICEF estimates that the death rate of children aged under five in Madagascar stood at 126 per 1000 in 2003.

Long-term Immersion Among the Excluded

Before launching a program committing the ATD Fourth World Movement, Chantal Laureau worked as a doctor with the Missionaries of Charity Brothers for two years. During this time, she got to know the country, found out about the health situation and listened to the sick during checkups. When the neighborhood where the program was to be implemented was chosen, she got further involved in the life of the very poor, meeting them in their homes for long periods, spending hours listening to them to discover their hopes, strengths and sufferings, and then writing for hours about these discoveries to completely familiarize herself with them and to keep a record. It was only after several years that the mothers dared to disclose their concerns and practices, especially their use of traditional remedies. Knowledge is built on action that, in turn, creates new opportunities for knowledge. The very fact that these people are visited where they live is of great significance to the value they are given: "Nobody had ever come to our home, except for you" some mothers said. This reinforces their self-esteem and therefore their capabilities.

Cultural Action to Strengthen People's Capabilities

Despite the efforts made by the inhabitants to take care of their children and make up for all that is lacking, they are often seen as incompetent, ignorant and unable to develop. They too come to see their situation as hopeless. Hence, any proposal for development seems destined for others. Action teams have to take into account this crucial reality, an intrinsic part of the heritage of the very poor and of their "truncated" culture. Therefore, any action aimed at empowering them must include a strong cultural dimension that is essential for the people, their families and the community itself. It is also essential to help the poorest express their aspirations, not only their concerns, and to join them in their aspirations.[63] The community must be able to gradually develop into a collective player and partner associated in defining and implementing action to improve everybody's well-being. We have seen how the ATD Fourth World team has acted at these different levels by being very close to the people and a part of their neighborhood, which is an essential factor. An ongoing theme throughout the program was the desire to strengthen solidarity within the neighborhood.

Organizing a Meeting Between Two Different Worlds

In 1997, after six years of work in the neighborhood, the ATD Fourth World team felt they were now able to organize meetings between parents and health care professionals, without running the risk of parents being put down or ridiculed by the professionals. The team itself had gained the trust of the parents and of the medical staff. It was sufficiently known by both parties to be considered as a trusted mediator. The mothers had acquired the appropriate language skills and a certain oral ability by speaking among themselves and with this health team about their young children. They had started to fill in the development books, which they could show as a clear sign of the interest they give to the development of their children. Nevertheless, the place and time must be carefully chosen so that people belonging to very

---

63. More guidelines for action can be found in *Reaching the Poorest*, by UNICEF and ATD Fourth World, 1999, available at UNICEF.

different worlds can meet productively. These meetings must take place away from any medical care center, so as not to recreate stressful conditions in which the parents arrive late and make the medical staff feel they have failed. It is important for the parents to meet medical staff from various departments so that they can visit these departments and understand how they work. It is important that the medical staff can meet the parents in premises in their neighborhood, around the parents' questions and concerns, and that they understand the real effort made for their children's well-being. We have seen that this type of meeting can lead to a real "U-turn" in the attitude of health care staff—from an attitude of distrust and rejection to one of understanding and support. The person experiencing such a U-turn then becomes the main door through which Antohomadinika inhabitants pass to access health care. Beyond informal knowledge sharing with work colleagues, that person can also use his room to manoeuvre to ensure a long-term relationship between the institution and the very poor. The creating of a permanent space within the institution where the poorest customers can be heard is undoubtedly the best way to achieve this.

Inventing a New Language by Merging Different Types of Knowledge

There are more than enough words to talk about extreme poverty. More often than not, they are used in monologs by people from the same social background and not in a dialog between people from different backgrounds. Everyday language relating to the very poor overflows with humiliating phrases, of which the most often heard is that if they live like that, "It's because they want to." The language employed by economists, sociologists, doctors or other experts in the field of poverty tries to avoid value judgments, but it is often incomprehensible to those who live in poverty. All too often, the language used by experts dehumanizes poverty by turning real people into nothing but technical problems or statistics. To ensure communication between health care professionals and poverty stricken families, a suitable language must be invented which respects both those who exclude and those who are excluded.

> This is a real art, or rather a craft, to find words that neither deny suffering nor condemn anyone. The words must remain true to the gravity of the issue, yet humiliate no one. They must reestablish the dignity of the excluded while opening a path to those who exclude. This new language confronts without condemning, enabling each one to express oneself and learn from others.[64]

In the account of the program undertaken in Antohomadinika, this language must face up to the challenge of conciliating the experience-based knowledge of the mothers and the professional knowledge of the medical staff, traditional Madagascan knowledge and Western knowledge. A fundamental aim of this new language is to allow each person to understand and learn from another person.

The book, *Our children are a treasure*, succeeds in combining two forms of knowledge: one a result of a harsh life where you always have to be on your toes to survive and another which is more academic, which can take a step back but is often unaware of the constraints present in the lives of the very poor. This new common language, which acknowledges

---

64. Jona M. Rosenfeld & Bruno Tardieu, "Artisans of Democracy", University Press of America, 2000 p. 228.

the importance of the Madagascan community's traditions and those of Western medicine, gives rise to a new way in which people come together and to forms of knowledge which are no longer used as elements of power by one group over another but as complements to one another where ideas can grow. In the account in question, this new language was created by the neighborhood's inhabitants through the gradual disclosure of their knowledge with the ATD Fourth World team. This knowledge later met with that of other health care professionals and academic knowledge. This is clearly a bottom-up approach. A top-down approach appears to be totally unsuitable to merging different types of knowledge as it would be based on academic knowledge, which the very poor know nothing about and which would only convince them of being incapable of making any worthwhile contribution.

Training Matrons: Other Training Policies for Health Care Staff

The dead end in which the inhabitants of Antohomadinika and the medical care staff found themselves at the beginning of this account certainly raises questions on medical training given in the Third World. Madagascan hospital staff are trained according to the principles of Western medicine, while the situation on the ground is radically different. In addition to the numerous difficulties mentioned in this account, another well known consequence of this approach is a brain drain to Northern countries, particularly that of doctors and nurses attracted by the far bigger salaries and better work conditions offered there. Some of these countries do not train enough medical staff to meet their own needs and therefore do not hesitate in organizing recruitment campaigns for medical staff trained in the South. According to the World Bank, some 80,000 highly qualified people leave Africa annually to work overseas,[65] among which are many physicians and nurses,[66] and "the brain drain from developing to industrial countries will be one of the major forces shaping the landscape of the twenty first century". The aims laid down by the World Health Organization for Southern countries, to have in the year 2000 one doctor per 5000 inhabitants and one qualified nurse per 1000 inhabitants, were not reached in 38 sub-Saharan countries.[67] Western countries have an average of one doctor per 500 inhabitants but do not hesitate to recruit those who were trained in the South! Reversing this trend very clearly involves radical changes to the medical staff training policies both in the North and in the South.

We have seen the very important role played by matrons in the Antohomadinika neighborhood. Would it not be possible to set up training programs for matrons, who are a lot closer to the inhabitants than the hospital staff and a lot less likely to escape their country and emigrate to the north? These programs should harmonize the wealth of traditional Madagascan medicine and medical traditions and the contributions of Western medicine.

---

65. Quoted in *World Migration 2003*, report by the International Organization for Migrations, p 215 and 217. This figure does not include the many students who study overseas.

66. Physicians for Human Rights state that Zambia's public sector retained only 50 of the 600 physicians that have been trained in the country's medical school from approximately 1978 to 1999. www.phrusa.org/campaigns/aids.

67. Cécile Bontron, *Le Monde* newspaper, June 28, 2005, "African brain drain northwards."

CHAPTER 5

Taking the Time to Learn
from the Poor in Tanzania

Niek Tweehuysen and Andrew Hayes[68]

*When a team from the Fourth World Movement first arrived in Tanzania, its
mission was summed up in two challenges: "When we find the friends of the
poorest of the poor, we want to learn from their experience. When we find
the poorest of the poor who have no friends, we want to find friends with
them." This chapter tells the story of how the team encountered and learned
from the very poor.*

In our mission, as members of the Tanzanian team of the Fourth World Movement,
we often speak of "people who suffer from living in poverty." Many people we meet
consider themselves poor, but at the same time they are often able to overcome the
difficulties of their lives thanks to strong family ties, strong relationships within their community or help from friends. Little by little, we have gotten to know the country as a place
where people help each other, and where the friends of the poor are the Tanzanian people themselves. People help others and they in turn will be helped if necessary. We have
witnessed many such gestures. While these gestures may not be witnessed by those who
do not share the life of the poor, they are offered without any desire for praise or any

68. This chapter was written by the Tanzania team of the International Movement ATD Fourth World
under the coordination of Niek Tweehuysen and Andrew Hayes. It was first published as a self-standing
document of the International Movement ATD Fourth World, 2003, *Three Years of Learning in Tanzania*,
Pierrelaye and Dar es Salaam. The document was edited for this publication by Rahel Kassahun and
Quentin Wodon and is printed here with the permission of the International Movement ATD Fourth
World. The views expressed in this chapter are those of the authors, and they do not necessarily represent
those of the World Bank, its Executive Directors, or the countries they represent.

demand for a favor in return, simply as part of the natural responsibilities of being a member of a community or a family.

At the same time however, we have also witnessed the plight of some among the poorest of the poor who may not be able to rely on others because their family and community are themselves so poor that they don't have much that they can share. In getting to know these communities, we have been able to feel the suffering that these people go through every day. We have had to ask ourselves the question of "how is it that these communities, the poorest and those that are wealthier, are able to live side by side and yet never really seem to meet?"

Learning about the lives of those who suffer the most from living in poverty has shocked some and raised many questions for others. One friend said during a meeting:

> Before, when I went to the fish market, I went to look for fish but now I have learned to look at the market in a different way. Now I have learned to pay attention to the one who is selling or cleaning the fish.

In this chapter, we would like the reader to get to know some of these people and what they think about their life. We will also try to highlight some of the activities that we have organized and how the international character of such events has been helpful in linking those suffering from living in poverty with the outside world. Most of all, we would like to explain what we have learned from these activities and why we organized them in the first place.

Encountering the Very Poor

From our rented house and small office in Mwananyamala, we have lived our daily life together with the local population. This has resulted in friendships with a large number of them and these friendships have helped us to better understand the challenges that families face in trying to raise their children and live a decent life. We have been able to observe those children who go to school and those who do not, the young people who have work and those who have nothing else to do but to sit and wait in their neighborhoods all day long. We have gotten to know the condition of the houses in which people live, with a whole family living in a single room, with parents, children and all a family's possessions exposed to heat, rain, and other elements.

We have felt the anger of people when they have caught a thief and witnessed how this anger can boil over into mob justice. We have experienced life in a big town, with the interruptions in the supply of water and electricity, and the difficulties of the transport system. We have observed an army of girls living away from their homes and often working just for food, so lonely that they end up roaming the streets in the evening looking for some affection and the boy or man of their dreams. We have visited, and buried some of our own friends affected by diseases such as malaria and HIV/AIDS. Our "friends around the house" have helped us to better understand the suffering with which these people live. Our friends have also taken us to places and helped us to communicate with the local people both in Dar es Salaam and around the country. They have supported us a great deal, explaining to our neighbors our work and our intentions.

We have made weekly visits to the fish market in Dar es Salaam, where many people live and work in difficult conditions. We have come to know some of these people over the past three years and held meetings with them in Kigamboni where they have spoken about their lives and how to reach out to those who suffer even more than they do. A number of these meetings have been prepared and chaired by members of this group, and one friend has been prominent in this process. He lives and works at the market and knows many, if not most, of those who work there, especially the young people who rely on small jobs such as cleaning fish and washing cars.

We have met people in other parts of Dar es Salaam and its surrounding areas, where families work together in the quarry beside the road leading to Bagamoyo, as well as families living along Morogoro Road who had to leave their homes to make way for the extension and widening of the road. We have also tried to understand the lives of those we have met in other parts of Dar es Salaam which carry a bad reputation, such as Uwanja wa Fisi or Kariakoo.

Beyond Dar es Salaam, we have learned a great deal through our travels to all but two regions of the country. People who had been in contact with us through the "Permanent Forum: Extreme Poverty in the World" and people that we came to know through these visits in different parts of the country often led us to other areas, sometimes remote places, where we found people suffering from drought, hunger and lack of education or health facilities.

We met with families living, almost autonomously, in little villages far away from the "outside world" and we were able to live with some of them for a short period of time. We were also privileged enough to travel with some of the young people that we know from the fish market in Dar es Salaam, embarking on travels that reunited them with their families, sometimes after as much as ten years or more apart. These travels meant that the young people had to face up to some tough questions, such as "why had they run away or left home in the first place?" and "why it had taken so long for their relation with their parents or their wider family to be restored?" What we have learned from these instances and examples continues to be reflected upon and exchanged with others in the hope that we can all deepen our understanding of extreme poverty.

Regularly visiting people where they live helped us to better understand their lives. One member of the team discovered a group of families living in beached ships that were later to be sold as scrap. It was possible to reach these people only at low tide. Through repeated visits, the team member was introduced to other people squatting in these shipwrecked remains. Many children living there had been dismissed from overcrowded centers which cater to children living on the streets. One of the men there had suffered from a bout of typhoid and three bouts of malaria fever over a short period of time. He described his efforts to find a job this way:

> I have worked a whole day for just a meal as compensation. I have been lured into working for free, expecting to be hired longer if I worked well....Other people pretend that we are content with staying here, but what do they really know? Do you know that we dream of living in a real house?

Examples such as these reveal some of the faces of the social, and often physical, isolation that is distinctive of extreme poverty. They show the many challenges facing the most excluded individuals, families and communities who must fight every day for their dignity and survival. While trying to make ends meet, they make unstinting efforts to help preserve their family links and guarantee the future of their children. Their acts of resilience and courage often go unnoticed—like those mothers who resort to begging to gather the amount due for school fees and school supplies, putting into practice their aspiration for a better future for their children so that, as they often say, "our children will not have to go through what we have experienced ourselves."

It takes time to meet the very poor and to really understand what they must go through in their live. This can be illustrated through the testimony of a young missionary, whom we met through a trusted Tanzanian friend who is a member of the Society of Missionaries of Africa, known as the White Fathers. This young White Father stayed with us for one year, renting a little room not far away from our own house. After the completion of his year with us, he held a meeting with the Archbishop of Dar to discuss the important role that religious communities can and do play in the fight against poverty. He wrote the following about the experience he gained:

> It takes time to learn of the true suffering of your neighbor. The poor want to walk with their heads held high, like everybody else. Many families in the house I live in do not have much to live on. Even the landlady would come to me to explain how she finds it hard to pay the school fees for her daughter. It took me five months to find out that the children who used to greet me with respect every day were almost starving. Their mother had died and their father was working extra hours to pay the debt he had acquired trying to save the life of his wife. He would leave very early in the morning and come back very late at night. I rarely saw him. One night I heard crying coming from their tiny room. I forced the door open and found that the elder brother, Haji, had tied the twins to the bed and was flogging them. The reason was that the previous day one of them, while carrying a pot of soup, had slipped and spilt it on the ground. They had not eaten since then.
>
> I could have helped the landlady keep her daughter in college. She came to me, begging, although she had a house and she was able to send her daughter to a private school. Neither Haji nor his father ever came to me to ask for help. They always greeted me with a happy face and yet they had nothing to eat for a full day. Haji could not finish primary school. His younger twin sisters were about to stop going to school because they had no uniforms. The landlady had cut off the electricity to their room and they were banned from fetching water from the house tap because they could not pay the bills. For months Haji had taken up the responsibilities of a parent. He sometimes went far away to beg for help. He is tough. He had to be tough. Is there a way of letting the landlady see her relative poverty through the eyes of Haji? How can someone help Haji maintain his independence and enhance his initiative? It will not be right for me to think that I know what poverty is and how to eradicate it after knowing someone like Haji. I cannot but admire his courage.

We were privileged through our contact and work with this young priest to learn how the Tanzanian people see the isolation of other members of society. It often astonished us that the knowledge of such realities did not seem to penetrate deep into society, and that such realities really had to be, and still have to be, discovered. One concern that this young priest had was to find ways to address this problem. One way that he found to do this was to speak of what he was learning to those communities he knew and that could be said to be "more privileged."

Simply placing himself in such an environment, sharing the life that came with that environment and the house that he lived in, brought him a new understanding of the life around him and stands as an example of how it is possible for one person to open himself up to the lives of others. This also inspires more Tanzanians to find their own way to meet, live with and work within such excluded communities in the future. Such a commitment could possibly lead to more Tanzanians joining the Movement and becoming members of the international volunteer corps.

Box 5.1 provides the testimony of Paul, a young man from Dar es Salaam. Reading what Paul wrote made us think a lot. Even with all that he had been going through in his years on the streets, he could still make us think about the meaning of identity. He had concrete propositions for actions, and he described the conditions in which those living in poverty can give voice to their hopes. Paul is 22 years old now, and has great difficulty picturing a future for himself, but the difficult conditions in which he lives do not prevent him from being a spokesman for others. We are now beginning to understand what might be behind what some young people said to us during one meeting: "Yes, we want to help you to find people who are even poorer than ourselves but do not forget that we

---

Box 5.1: Paul

Paul came to see us to excuse himself. "I could not come on 17 October because I was in prison." He then told us the story of his arrest.

> With a number of friends, I was sleeping behind an enclosure on a piece of ground in the city center. I had been chased away from somewhere else and thought that I could sleep there without too many problems. But all of a sudden the police came and I found myself in prison. They accused us all of vagrancy.

Paul showed us the scars covering his body. He explained,

> Those who have been in prison for a long time can attack those who have just arrived. When I was taken to court and put in prison, the stronger inmates took from me the small amount of money that I had. I couldn't defend myself against them. My friend even lost his shoes to them. I am not proud of all of this but it is our life.

During a meeting with young people living on the streets of Dar es Salaam, Paul said, "We, the young people, must speak loud and clear. We must come together like a family to ensure the rights and responsibilities of each and everyone." Despite the fact that he was tired, we asked him to put down his experiences on paper and come up with propositions so that his life and that of his friends would improve. He worked hard to find the right words to explain what he wanted to say:

> Nobody chooses the place where they are born. It could be a place where life is hard or a place where life is more comfortable. For this reason we must all respect each other because we are all human. Millions of children live in very difficult conditions, some because they have lost their parents and some because of the poverty of their family. One of the consequences of this difficult life is that some of these children, at a very young age, will leave their town or village and start living a difficult life on the streets of big towns or cities like Dar es Salaam.
>
> They will look for small bits of work during the day and maybe they will find just enough for a plate of rice. Living this way is dangerous not just for their health but because they also risk being accused of stealing. Today we are seen as vagabonds and vagrants, and we risk being thrown into prison at any time, but we were born in this country and we want to do everything so as to earn a living legally. We wash cars, clean fish, even crush stones to make gravel. But many of us never went to school, so we don't know the rights that would protect us. We need our leaders to support us so that we can live freely. Time spent in prison is time that is lost. If we are taken and put in prison, and nobody knows where we are, then it is like we don't exist anymore. It is almost as if we don't have any identity.
>
> Everything starts with the family, where one should be able to live a decent life with good relationships. Good relationships with society will lead to good conduct. Parents can give moral training to their children so that they can have good relations with society. Together, knowing that we are all people, we can all strengthen humanity by respecting each other. We all know what we want for those that we are close to. Listening to and showing respect to them are a big support that can lift people out of their isolation. One can share ideas regardless of where someone comes from. We can overcome poverty when we live like a family. In this way the poor will not be ashamed of their situation but instead will feel supported and regain hope for the future.

also have a difficult life." For us, the question of how to best support Paul remains unanswered, but the fact that he was able to express himself as he did is, as he said, the start of the creation of that big family of which he is dreaming.

Enabling the Very Poor to Join Forces

In 1980, Joseph Wresinski, the founder of the Movement, wrote a letter to friends all over the world who were in contact with the Movement. This letter explained that

> for a number of years now, we have been trying to establish a network of all those who want to fight extreme poverty on the different continents. We have given this network the name, the "Permanent Forum: Extreme Poverty in the World." Today we want to transform the individual contacts that we have into a platform of permanent exchange where everybody can both speak of their own experiences and hear the experiences and the reflections of others. Our exchange will consolidate the solidarity between people who carry the same conviction to liberate the poorest, who are excluded from the hope of a better life and from participation in the world around them.

Today, 40 people in Tanzania receive the newsletter "Letter to Friends around the World" from the international office of the Movement in France. This letter is a means of communication among members of the "Permanent Forum: Extreme Poverty in the World," which itself aims to bring together individuals, NGOs, and national and international organizations to the common fight against poverty, while at the same time respecting their independence of these different organizations. While the forum reaches out to many people all over the world, the fact that we are only a small team in Tanzania has meant that we have had to focus on building a stronger foundation for the Movement here in Tanzania. To build this foundation we have held meetings of the "Friends of the Movement" in Dar es Salaam, at both our house and at our office, bringing together people with a desire to share their own experiences and strengthen the future of the Movement in the country. These meetings have also afforded us the opportunity to foster a common understanding of the Movement, its structure and the heritage of Joseph Wresinski.

We also write a national newsletter that we send to more than one hundred and fifty friends in Tanzania, Kenya and Uganda. Most of these friends have a long-standing commitment to the poor in their community and region. After receiving the national newsletter, one person wrote:

> Thank you for the letters that you forward to us regularly. It is good to feel that you are not so far away from us, and I remain very touched by your activity. Despite all the problems that you face and witness, you remain so positive that it encourages people, like us here, who sometimes forget to trust the weakest.

Our trips to various regions of Tanzania were taken in part to allow young people who worked in the fish market of Dar es Salaam to break out of their immediate surroundings and isolation. This led among others to a series of meetings in Kigamboni. These meetings helped the young people understand that they are not alone in their situation and that we can all represent and support each other. When the group read a letter written in October 2000 by young people in contact with the Movement in Peru, they immediately wanted to write back.

First of all, we thank all the young people in Peru for remembering others who live the same life that they do. We are not tired of hearing your story and we hope you are not tired of hearing about our lives. When we read your letter we thought we must write back to you. We want to exchange [ideas and experiences] because our lives are the same. It is only the country that is different. We ask you to come together so that we can fight for the rights of those who would have liked to live and grow up at home, but problems made them run away. You are suffering from the cold, but let us come together and banish poverty. Like you, we have a difficult life. Like you, we do any type of work: we clean cars and we fetch firewood for those who fry fish. At night, we have no place to sleep. Sometimes we live like birds. But we believe God will save us and that one day we will meet together, if it is not in this world, then in the next, in Heaven. But today we cannot forget our relatives and families.

We hope to continue to hear from you, so that we can help each other to escape from the tough conditions we live in. We would like to buy you a small gift from Tanzania, but it might not be possible because we have no money. But we would like to try. We have made a promise to look for people who have a more difficult life than we do. We promise to continue to come together, peacefully, the financially poor and the richest ones. Thank you again for your message. We love the youth of Peru, God bless Peru.

Two Tanzanian friends traveled to take part in gatherings in Mauritius and France. One of them attended the seminar "Reaching the Poorest Children," which was organized by the Movement in collaboration with UNICEF and the Government of Mauritius in April 2000. The seminar allowed members of the "Permanent Forum: Extreme Poverty in the World" from countries in the Indian Ocean to gather and exchange their thoughts, their ideas and their experiences on reaching out to the poor. The second participated in the General Assembly of the International Movement ATD Fourth World, held in France in January 2002. After the meeting, she explained that:

One of the most obvious impacts of the Movement's presence in the country is the fact that I have been able to go to France for this meeting. By being represented at this meeting, Tanzania is going to be known by people from many different countries. I have been able to learn from the different experiences of other countries and share something from Tanzania. With the Movement in our country we are going to be able to know the most disadvantaged groups.

In Mwananyamala, a group of young men who are fathers themselves visit us regularly. We have gotten to know their families and relatives, helping us to understand daily life in Dar es Salaam. These young workers have become our ambassadors in the neighborhood but, little by little, a number of them have also become strong supporters of the Movement and have accompanied us on many occasions. Their familiarity with the neighborhood has provided security for the team members, who are vulnerable because of their status as outsiders and foreigners living in an area that, for many people, carries a bad reputation and is assumed to be unsafe.

International Day for the Eradication of Poverty

In our work, one question remains paramount: "How can solidarity with people living in extreme poverty be exercised on a permanent basis and what would this solidarity look like?" One occasion which seeks to bring people together is the "International Day for the Eradication of Poverty." Celebrated every year on October 17th, and officially recognized by the United Nations' General Assembly in 1992, this day was first organized by the Movement in 1987. Today, with the collaboration of various NGOs, the day is an invitation to the public at large to hear the voice of people living in poverty and encourage all members of society to consider ways in which they can contribute to the fight against poverty. We have commemorated the day each year, with more and more people attending the event and joining the celebration of the day.

On the occasion of the very first celebration of this day in Tanzania, one of our friends wrote a strong but simple message that was later broadcasted worldwide: "I have to congratulate you with the celebration for 17 October. Everybody has to fight and fight again because poverty is a danger to mankind." This idea that "poverty is a danger for mankind" is the very message of the International Day for the Eradication of Poverty. It is not a day only for those who know poverty but for everybody, and a day where many different groups, organizations and people stand side by side with the poorest people of society. Over the past three years groups from as far away as Iringa, Moshi, and Bagamoyo have participated in the celebrations that we have held to mark the day, making the day one that reflects more and more the realities of Tanzania as a whole.

A number of groups from Dar have also supported the day with their presence. The Tanzanian Albino Society has spoken of their struggle for life and for respect and how they try to search for the poorest of the poor and the most excluded among their community. The "Child in the Sun" center has sent a delegation to show their commitment not only to homeless young people to whom they offer professional training, but also to tackling the root causes that bring so many young people to a life on the streets. The Unemployed Single Women Program has presented the difficulties that women face when raising a family on their own and how, despite these difficulties, they still invest their hopes in a future of work for themselves and schooling for their children. Members of Youth Alive Club, young people trying to counsel their own generation in youth groups or in schools of the dangers of HIV/AIDS, have also participated.

Some of our friends have marked the event by gathering other friends and organizations in the spirit of the day. We hope that in the future we can spread this symbolic gesture of coming together around the message voiced by Joseph Wresinski on that very first celebration of the day back in 1987: "Wherever men and women are condemned to live in poverty, human rights are violated. To come together to ensure that these rights be respected is our solemn duty."

The day is an opportunity to restate and renew our commitment to the poorest and to express the hope that we will remain close to the poorest in our own communities throughout the rest of the year. This is a commitment and a hope that can then be seen at other times which carry a great significance, such as Christmas. For the last three years, along with a youth group in Dar, we have organized a festive celebration around Christmas with young people from the fish market. Members of the youth group come in large numbers each time, to perform theatre sketches and sing with the young people of the fish market. The aim has always been for such celebrations to initiate contact between the young people of both groups and to create a better understanding of each others' lives not just at Christmas but also throughout the year.

A second global event that we have celebrated is the International Day of the Family. On May 15th, we celebrate this day by asking our strongest supporters to invite their spouses, children and mothers to come together. This offers a rare escape from daily chores of cooking, fetching water, washing and looking after children. There is joy in being able

---

Box 5.2: Andrew

Two years ago, Mudi, one of the young men living at the fish market, had been in prison for a number of months when one of his friends spoke to a team member about him.

> Mudi has been in prison for such a long time now, but he still hasn't been convicted of anything. There hasn't been a trial and we don't know what he has been charged with. The others who were taken at the same time have all been released but he is still in there because he has no relatives to fight for him.

A friend of the Movement left with one of the young men from the fish market and together they tried to find their friend. When they finally found Mudi, he was very weak as he had lost weight, developed problems with his eyesight and was suffering from a skin infection and a bout of malaria. Soon after this visit, he was released and went back to the fish market.

Once back at the market, Mudi spoke about his life in prison and the difficulties he had faced there. He also spoke about another young man, Andrew, maybe only fifteen or sixteen years old, who was in prison. Mudi told us that Andrew was so ill that he was afraid Andrew might die. We decided to visit him and Mudi came with us. We found Andrew who was indeed very ill. We managed to have him admitted to a hospital. A few days later, he passed away. We decided to bury Andrew but the team had never before organized a funeral. We had to rely entirely on the young people from the fish market and some of the friends around us. Friends arranged for formalities with the hospital and the police to be taken care of. Once this was done, we tried to mobilize as many people as we could to give Andrew a decent funeral. With the young people of the fish market, our friends from Mwananyamala and other members of the community in attendance, Andrew was buried with a simple ceremony and a great deal of emotion. We then promised each other to do everything that we could in the future to fight the loneliness and the isolation of some of our friends.

The International Day for the Eradication of Poverty is an occasion to reaffirm this commitment by thinking of those who are left behind or alone. It is for this reason that we visit the grave of Andrew on this day each year, not only to remember him and all the work that went into organizing a decent burial for him, but to renew the promise that we made to each other.

---

to share time together, as a family, away from the difficulties of live. This day has become a celebration not only of the family but also of efforts that go into keeping a family together. Fighting poverty is fighting for families. As Joseph Wresinski noted "The family is the first defense against poverty."

Other Sources of Knowledge

A friend came to us one day and explained how one young girl in his extended family was in danger of being excluded from school since the family had not been able to pay her school fees. A family meeting had decided that everybody should contribute 5000TSh (Tanzanian Shillings) to cover the cost of the fees and keep the girl in school. The problem for our friend was that at the end of a work day, he would have only 600TSh left in his pocket. It would have taken him two weeks, maybe more, to be able to contribute so much. Earning so little, and knowing that his family was aware of this, he assumed that he was exempt from contributing. As the date neared for the members of his family to produce their contributions, our friend suddenly found out that he was not exempt at all, and was expected to contribute like everybody else in his family.

We have encountered many similar situations, witnessing both the aspirations of the very poor and also their difficulties in contributing to, and investing in. what is most important in their lives: education, health and the family. The efforts of the poor themselves are crucial, but others contribute as well. We have tried to find as many individuals, groups and organizations who are committed to the fight against poverty as possible, so as to learn from their knowledge and the realities that they face. One forum that we found was the *Poverty Reduction Strategy Paper (PRSP)*, published by the Tanzanian Government, and the emphasis that it placed on going to the heart of the issue. This plan asked explicitly for the very poor and other stakeholders in society to assist in the evaluation of poverty alleviation in the country.

The PRSP inspired the Poverty Policy Week held in Dar in September 2002. The Vice-President of the United Republic of Tanzania opened the meeting by placing

> ... due emphasis on the issue of empowerment to enable the poor to have influence over and ownership of the decisions which concern their livelihood and have a direct impact on their living conditions.

The meeting highlighted that the regions which ranked at the bottom of the development scale were rural areas such as Lindi and Shinyanga. So, what does it mean to speak of fighting poverty for a team such as ourselves that is based in an urban area? Such information has only served to strengthen the team's desire to deepen its contact with those actors working in such remote areas and introduce them to a whole new circle of friends and network of support.

The team also participated in meetings, organized by UNESCO, on the subject of Education for All. The Regional Consultation of NGOs and CSOs Working in Education in Africa in Lilongwe, Malawi in September 2002 and the Eighth Conference of Ministers of Education of African Member States in Dar in December 2002 presented an opportunity to give voice to some of the realities and situations that we have come to know in Tanzania. The issue of school fees discussed earlier may have been resolved by the government's directive that abolished all fees, but there are still other obstacles which prevent people from accessing their right to education.

The team has invested in the education of some young men in an effort to better understand the necessary conditions to reach targets such as those stated in the Education for All initiative. One young man that we know wanted to learn English, but the timetable for classes clashed with his work at a local market, meaning that he would not be present to help close the market stall or help transport goods away from the market at the end of the day. His enrollment in the class could entail not just a loss of work and money, but also possible resentment from those who would now have to do his share of the work. Still, his friends and colleagues encouraged him to continue with his English course, dividing his work between themselves as their contribution towards his education. Without such support, his attendance would have been impossible.

To understand better what such support means and how it is formed, we embarked upon a project from which we hoped everybody would learn. We invited some friends to learn English, knowing that there would be other battles to wage to succeed apart from simply studying a new language. A number of these friends had only one year or less of primary education, so we had to confront the conditions necessary to facilitate the re-entry of young adults into the education system. We also had to confront the shame of being in a classroom

---

Box 5.3: Saidi

Pemba is an island of Zanzibar. It is Ramadan and it is possible to feel what this means on an island where ninety-five per cent of the population is Muslim. As a non-Muslim, it is amazing to see a whole population, for one month, neither eating nor drinking, not even drinking water from morning to evening. This requires discipline even if the meal at night can be substantial, if one can afford it. Even those who know what it is like to be hungry try to observe the fast, but one can imagine the difficulties this represents for those who have little strength. Ramadhan is a time to think of all those who have little, a time to learn what it means to be hungry and thirsty. Perhaps the rich and poor feel united during this month as they embark on the same effort. But to feel united there must be in the first place a community that knows one another.

Saidi manages to feed himself with what he earns from the small work that he finds during the day. Because he has not been able to bury his father and his grandfather, due to only belatedly finding out that they had died, and not having the means to return home, he is in a very difficult position psychologically and often acts as if he is insane. He drinks water from shallow holes in the earth, he no longer dresses himself correctly, and has been found writing incomprehensible graffiti on walls.

Some of his friends took him by force, binding his wrists together, to see a man who reads the Koran in front of him. This calmed him down. Saidi now believes that he must go and visit the grave of his father to truly heal himself. It was a witchdoctor, if we understood correctly, who gave him this advice. Saidi wanted to observe Ramadhan but it wasn't possible. He managed to observe the fast for a few days, but then his resolve cracked. In the end, Saidi had to break the Ramadhan fast. We can sense that this has caused him a great deal of suffering, and he knows that we care. Perhaps knowing this is one of the reasons why Saidi continues to get up every morning filled with new hope. However, it leaves us asking ourselves the question "how can we increase the number of people who can sense the sufferings of the poorest like Saidi?"

We must fight to build this community life that we witnessed in Pemba where everybody seemed to count, to be known and to be recognized, so that we can all support each other. Yet, this was a community that was not there to come to support Saidi in his efforts to earn a place in Heaven. But we cannot believe that he has missed his chance for a piece of Heaven. The challenge of "giving the best of oneself before one dies" is very real in this context and is a message which must speak to all who have been involved in this effort for Ramadhan.

---

with a teacher and other students when one has difficulties to read and write properly. It was only through friendship and the will to support each other that we learned how it was possible to overcome such obstacles.

Another source of information was our participation in the *United Nations World Summit on Sustainable Development* in Johannesburg, South Africa in August 2002 where, as was the case in the UNESCO meetings, we represented the international arm of the Movement. We were able to make new friends there and, through the report submitted to the summit that we presented in a number of meetings, we were able to share some of our experiences in Tanzania. One team member traveled to the summit, accompanied by one of our friends from Mwananyamala. For our friend, the chance to witness and participate in such a meeting was an incredible opportunity, while for the team member, our friend's presence was invaluable in revealing just what such a meeting could mean for Tanzania and the communities that were the intended beneficiaries of the summit. The team organized a meeting in Tanzania where the experiences and the thoughts that came from the summit were shared with the young people of the fish market.

The friend who had traveled to Johannesburg to support the team found upon his return to Dar that he had lost his job. This again points to the great risks that the poor must take in order to represent themselves and others when they have very little protection at their workplaces.

The media, especially the newspapers, have played another key role in our understanding of the country. We have cut stories from the newspapers on what we understand to be the most important issues facing the country. We have done this to compare the national discourse with the experience gaining in living with our friends in Mwananyamala, Dar and other regions across the country. These cuttings now form an archive that is there to be studied and shared with others. From all of our sources of information, we have attempted to gather data on three subjects: education, health and the family. We have done this in the hope that what we learn about these subjects can become a tool to bring us together with other individuals and groups committed to the fight against poverty, and allow us to focus on areas where we can work together. Our aim has always been to learn from the efforts being made by others in the country towards poverty eradication, in the hope that sharing knowledge about these efforts with the people most concerned, the poorest themselves, can lead to a better future for all.

Partners in Development

We never had the intention of coming into the country and immediately starting a project. Our first concern was always to learn from the experiences of others about the country, its culture and its history. To do this would mean gathering people with experience in order to learn from them, but this would have to be part of an exchange. We therefore also wanted to share our own experiences and what we were learning, and we wanted others to get to know the history of the Movement and its founder. Such exchanges were not always easy, and there were many expectations and ideas that we could not live up to.

During one meeting where such experiences were being shared, among those present were a dozen young people from the fish market and a former government employee. The young people spoke openly about their difficulties to make ends meet, their lack of education and their desire to live a better life. Our friend, the former government employee, listened to their stories and concluded by saying,

> If we want people to know the Movement, then we must start with these young people and support them to get what it is that they are asking for. When we succeed with them, all the people will know what the Movement does, and that it has concrete solutions for poverty.

This proposition was applauded by the young people and the team found itself in the difficult position of having to emphasize the central thrust of its mission: that of first learning from those people who have a strong commitment to the poorest, and then finding friends with the poor. Had we agreed to work solely with this small group of a dozen young people, all our energy would have been taken up by them to the exclusion of everything else. How could we reconcile our mission and this proposition? The team's response had to be that only with the mobilization of people all across the country would there be an answer to extreme poverty.

It was with this idea in mind that one year later, in June 2002, ten young people from the fish market left for the north of the country. They went to Moshi to support the ongoing renovation of a dormitory at a school for blind children. One of the friends of the Movement, a teacher at the school, had found it difficult to muster strong hands to finish the last stage of the renovation work. We put the proposal of going to Moshi to answer the teacher's call to the young people and they all responded positively. Today these young people continue to reflect on their experience in Moshi, on what this experience means to them, and on what this experience means to their community. Three views:

> I was very happy to go to Moshi because we went there to support people who face their own difficulties. Without such a reason, we could not have gone. I was happy to meet people who have their own problems and it made me feel stronger to be together with a group that took me outside of the life I know and live. We live in a difficult situation but we went there because we needed them to feel strong again, and for them to have the strength to face their difficulties. We may not have work or a place to sleep but we volunteered our efforts.
>
> When we came back to Dar, I felt good and I felt stronger. Even with the difficulties of our own life here, I kept thinking of the children in the school, of their life and of how we could continue to support them.
>
> We went there because of friendship, and because of a friendship that has existed for a long time. Without friendship nothing is possible. It is important to have respect for each and everyone in their life. Friends may argue and fight, but once the fighting finishes there is friendship again, and no matter where you go in the world you can never forget your friends.

The young people spent one week working on the renovations at the school, and at the end of that week the headmaster of the school paid his own tribute to them and the work that they had done. He said that the spirit that they had carried into their endeavor carried its own message for the community around the school and for the wider society. He told them:

> You have really shown us, by example, that you have come to work with the poor and not for the poor, and that poverty was created by man and therefore it is up to all of us to eradicate it by working together as a team. It is because of your moral commitment that I personally feel obliged to express my deep appreciation to you all…We shall make the community around us realize the importance of your help, so that they can join you in the fight to eradicate the problems pertaining to our school…It goes without saying that you have taken the pains and the sufferings of our pupils as your own, even though their sufferings are not of your creation. This teaches us the lesson that you care and that you recognize the difficulties that others face in their everyday life.

It might seem strange that our response to the difficulties that the young people face in their own lives was to encourage them to support others, but for us this was the only possible answer. The young people were able to voice their difficulties to us because we visited them and invited them to such meetings. Their isolation means that they have few people to turn to when they want to explain how it is that they live or when they want to campaign for something better. This is why proposing direct help, as our friend the former government employee did, is an obvious reaction.

Without holding the meeting, our friend might never have heard the voices of the young people from the fish market. This is why these meetings are important: they bring people from mainstream society together with those who are isolated or excluded to a forum where both can speak. It is the message of the Movement that it is only when the poorest work together with other members of society that progress can be made in fighting poverty. By working together, both the poorest and other sectors of society will be able to say that they have participated in this progress, and the poorest will be a real partner in their own development and that of the country.

The following example is one that highlights how powerful this partnership can be. The elder of identical twin brothers, both living and working at the fish market, came to us one day and asked us to speak to his younger brother. He had been troubled by his brother's behavior for some time: his brother had difficulty sleeping, and alcohol and drugs had taken their toll on his body and his mind. His brother was becoming a danger to both himself and to those around him. Having seen the elder twin approach us, other friends at the fish market joined him in expressing concerns. When we spoke to the younger twin, he said that all he wanted to do was to return home so that he could rest and recover. The friends of the twins then did all that they could to help make this a possibility. Neither twin had been home in almost ten years. They left with the company of one good friend and one member of the team. There was an incredible burst of emotion when the twins were finally reunited with their mother and their family after having been apart for so long.

The twins then stayed with their mother and their family in the village for a couple of months, giving the younger brother time to recover with the help of family life, village air and some work in the fields. Perhaps more time in such an environment would have helped him, but the twins decided to return to the market, returning not just to the work of cleaning and selling fish but also to the life of alcohol and drugs. Less than six months after his return to the fish market, came a moment when the danger that the younger twin posed to himself and to those around him became a reality. He and a friend, another fish cleaner, had a dispute over a small amount of money. In anger the younger twin took a knife, ever present at the market as tools for cleaning and gutting fish, and wielded it as a weapon. He stabbed his friend who died on the spot. The younger twin was swiftly set upon by an angry mob in revenge for the attack and had to be rescued by the police. He was arrested and then moved to the Central Police Station and later on to prison.

In response to this news, brought to us by young people from the fish market, we went to look for the elder twin brother and found him hiding in a small kiosk near the market. He was hiding, afraid for his own safety, because of his resemblance to his younger brother and his close link to him. He then stayed with us until he could return home with one member of the team and inform his family of what had happened. The family decided that he should come back to Dar, so that he could visit his younger brother in prison and check on his health. When we continued to visit the fish market, we discovered that the deceased had been a friend not just of many of the young people but of ours as well: Salum.

At the fish market we met some of Salum's friends and they mobilized themselves to escort us. One of them came with us to the hospital mortuary and identified Salum's body. Before the identification Salum had been entered in the hospital records as "unknown," but now his name was officially registered. From there, one of the young people accompanied us to the police station where we were granted permission to bury Salum. Friends at the fish market began to collect money to go towards the cost of the burial. One hundred and fifty people signed their names in a book, underneath a photo of Salum, signifying that despite the difficulties of their lives they had made a contribution.

It was only with such a mobilization of the young people and their active role in the organization of the funeral that the burial of Salum was made possible. And it was in tribute to this mobilization and organization that the funeral was attended by two hundred people who all came to pay their respects to the deceased and to his friends, with the ceremony being led by three Imams and directed by elders from our own neighborhood. The elder twin, out of respect for the deceased and those grieving for their friend, did not attend the funeral, but instead left messages for his friends at the fish market saying that he was now returning to his home village to start a new life. He had managed to visit his younger brother in prison, taking him some water and a small amount of food in the knowledge that such commodities might be scarce there.

Yet, the funeral is not the end for the young people of the fish market. They continue to search for members of Salum's family to inform them of his death and share their knowledge of him. It is not possible to document everything that has been learned from this tragedy, but a few key points stand out. Although Salum's death affected everybody at the fish market, there was no way for the young people there to raise the necessary funds for the funeral on their own. They could not bury Salum alone. This reality was made even more difficult to bear since the incident had been sensationalized by the media in the coverage given to this story, but still no individual or group from outside the market came to support them. Once more the isolation of the young people was apparent.

Once it was clear that there was support from outside of the market to ensure that Salum received a decent burial, the young people were able to mobilize themselves quickly. Even those who are often accused of bad behavior proved that they could be serious and display their humanity when the prevailing conditions allow such a gesture. The circumstances of Salum's death also revealed the reality of the life that many of these young people live. Many of them live without any piece of identification, meaning that if anything happens to them, it becomes very difficult to trace their family. One of the young people once confided that this situation meant that, "…you simply disappear." Such a "disappearance" may well have become Salum's fate, had the young people not had the courage to identify his body and fight for a decent burial.

We, as a team, also felt that it was important to be seen supporting both the friends of Salum and the twins. It was at this moment in time that the support that came from our friends was vital as they too worked hard to assist us in the organization of the funeral. It was this support from those around the team that allowed the neighbors and members of the community, including some we had not even met before, to come forward and be present at the ceremony. The presence of our friends, as well as that of our neighbors and the community, also meant that some of the isolation of the young people was broken. The presence of so many people—the team, the friends, the neighbors and the community—offered ample support to the young people, much of which they had never known existed before.

It is the team's consistent presence at the fish market that has allowed us to see the challenges that the young people face and the gestures that they make both to those outside of the market, as in the case of Moshi, and to each other, as in the case of ensuring a burial for Salum. It is through these gestures and actions that the young people prove that those living in poverty do not always wait to be supported, but are themselves capable of acting with and supporting others. This is the definition of partnership. Our hope is to be able to introduce the young people to new friends and other individuals, groups and organizations that could become their friends, because friendships that exist in the long term will be present to support the young people in times of distress and also share with them moments of great hope and joy.

Box 5.4: Hamis

For some months now, we have been reading in the newspaper, *The Guardian*, how a number of families have been living under the threat of being evicted from their homes. A major road, planned for several years, is being widened and the engineers have said that these houses are too close to the road. It is always traumatic for a family to have to leave their home but it is also clear that this road is important for the development of the country.

The residents were unsure of their position because of the contradictory statements that they received. One official assured them that the demolition exercise was to be halted for fear of affecting too many families, but still the bulldozers arrived. A number of youths tried to stop the constructors by throwing stones at a bulldozer and forcing the driver to flee in fear for his life, but the bulldozer returned the next day accompanied by officials who explained that the demolition had to take place. Against their will, the residents were left with no other choice but to leave, still hoping that their calls for compensation would be heeded. Up until the last moment, the residents tried to salvage what they could from their homes to help them build again. Some of the affected families took refuge in the homes of family members or friends, but others did not have this possibility. With all that they could carry, some headed for the office of the United Nations' High Commission for Refugees and camped outside the front door. The families then began to call themselves refugees.

Many people pitied them for their situation: the difficulties of living and sleeping outdoors with their children during the rainy season were obvious. But above all, this group of people camping outside such an institution was shameful for the officials who did not seem to be able to solve the situation in a more suitable way. With assistance of religious organizations and a large international organization, tents were procured. Some youth groups volunteered to help clear some waste ground and the tents were erected. The families were finally transported there from the UN offices by the police. The area is some forty kilometers from their old neighborhood. These tents are to house up to one hundred families, and the families can then claim a plot of land on another piece of waste ground nearby, on which they can then build a new house.

We went to see these families and after a long search we found the camp. Only twenty families lived there. It is almost impossible for them to do anything. There is no work in the area and no land to cultivate. All that is left to do is to wait for the sun to rise and wait for it to set. The families are fed by the local government. There is one water tap which, if everybody arrives, will have to serve up to six hundred people. The sanitary conditions are too harrowing to describe.

We met there Mama Aisha, her daughter Leila and her son Hamis. The father died several years ago, but before he died he had been able to build a small house for his family to guarantee them the security of always having a roof over their heads. "*I have lost everything,*" said Mama Aisha. Hamis said, "How can I work? I don't have the money to go back into town from here and even if I had it, I must stay here to protect my mother and sister." Leila said nothing but we know that she is no longer going to school. We shared a meal, sitting on the ground. We didn't know what to say to each other. There was a long silence. A number of those who have been evicted have been able to find some support, but Mama Aisha is in despair and there must be others like her.

The situation of these families leaves us with much to think about. The families have received support from organizations and other citizens, but is setting up a camp in the middle of the bush a real response to their distress? Organizations are bringing them food, but can this replace the work of Hamis? Can it replace Leila's schooling? The government assumed its responsibility when it provided the land for the tents and installed the water, but could it not have gone further? Could the foreign government providing funding for the road not have intervened?

Our own Movement was born in France in Noisy-le-Grand 1957 in a camp for those without homes. Africa is not Europe, but we are certain that the families of Noisy and the family of Mama Aisha, Leila and Hamis would understand each other. They would recognize each other through us, volunteers, and through members of the Movement all over the world. It is in this way that we are trying to build an International Movement that refuses to accept extreme poverty.

Conclusion

Looking back over the past three years, our presence here and our search to understand the country and its people have led us in a number of different directions. The primary aim of this search was always to try to find how Tanzanians contribute to the fight against poverty. It is through this search that we have come to the conclusion that the true friends of the poorest of the poor in Tanzania are the Tanzanian people themselves. The challenge we are thus faced with is that of remaining close to not only the very poor, but also those who stand side by side with them. It is these individuals, groups and organizations that must be encouraged to continue their commitment to, and their support of those with the most difficult lives. Neither these individuals, groups or organizations, nor the people and communities that they are committed to, can be allowed to feel isolated or excluded.

The way forward is to continue to look for the poorest of the poor who have no friends and to become friends with them. A study conducted jointly by the Movement and UNICEF, *Reaching the Poorest*, concluded that "poverty is in and of itself the greatest obstacle to reaching the poorest." Understanding this conclusion means recognizing that extreme poverty undermines family security and destroys social ties within a community. It prevents participation in development. It isolates and excludes its victims. To overcome these barriers we are looking for ways in which to experiment with one concrete project in a poor neighborhood around which both our friends and the community could unite and mobilize themselves. Some of our friends have already said that they want to be actively involved in such a project, which has meant investing in them so that they are able to acquire new skills and self-confidence. These new skills and self-confidence are the vital tools that our friends will need if they are to take the responsibility of such a project upon themselves and carry it out over a number of years. Among these friends are young people who have very little schooling and others who live or have lived in very difficult conditions, and it is this experience that will be invaluable. In making these young people our partners in this project, the experience that they carry with them guarantees that we will learn from them how Tanzanians reach out to the poorest and most excluded in their own society and how they stay close to them.

This experience, the experience of Tanzanian people in reaching out to the poorest, is not simply a case of witnessing the sufferings and exclusion of the poorest but also witnessing their struggle to overcome these sufferings. Friends have shown us on numerous occasions how the family is central to this struggle. To better understand the role that women and children play in the life of the family and the community, we hope to soon be able to facilitate a better communication with these groups through the presence of a female worker in the team. Such a presence will make it easier to learn how to build the conditions which allow people to take an active part in the process of poverty eradication by always asking for the participation of those who are hardest to reach out to, or those who suffer the most.

Having friends showing us the importance of the family has also been a key to understanding the lives of the people here and their own thoughts about their lives. Being close to them, whether here in Dar in other areas across the country, has enabled us to be present at some of the most important times of their lives, such as at times of illness, marriage, birth and mourning. In the process, we have come to appreciate the history of the country, its wisdom and its strength, and we see these lessons reflected in its people. It is with respect for these lessons that we have tried to involve Tanzanians in the organization, preparation and chairing of the meetings that we have held, and it is why we have often sought their advice and guidance in the face of difficult questions and difficult situations.

Our visits across the country have enabled us to make new friends who have welcomed the idea of supporting each other through the sharing of their experiences. These new friends have explained to us time and again how important it is for them to know that they are not alone in the struggle against poverty, that they can support others and that others can encourage them to continue to reach out to the most excluded in their own communities. However, in order for this exchange to work for the benefit of all, skills must be developed that can create the environment where such knowledge and experiences can be shared. In order to discover which conditions are necessary for this sharing to begin, we are still evaluating how to gain the most from those moments spent and shared together in working with people from different communities.

While facing all of these challenges in the years ahead, we want to continue to bear witness to the efforts of the Tanzanian people, both inside and outside of the Movement, to fight poverty and to reach out to those who are the poorest and most excluded. We want the country and its people to be recognized for their efforts and their hopes for a better future.

CHAPTER 6

Enabling Children to Learn in Latin America

*International Movement ATD Fourth World
(Bolivia, Guatemala, and Peru Teams)*[69]

> *The Fourth World Movement has teams in three Latin American countries:
> Guatemala, Peru, and Bolivia. This chapter provides contributions from these
> three teams. The Peru team focuses on its street library activities, the objective
> of which is to improve access to knowledge and education for poor children.
> The Guatemala team shares insights from the life of Doña Elena's family and
> children, as a way to better understand the difficulties which the very poor are
> confronted with and how they cope with these difficulties. The Bolivia team
> describes some activities from the Tapori network which aim to promote a better
> understanding among children from different socio-economic backgrounds.*

Reaching the Poorest Children Through Street Libraries in Peru

The creation of the Peru branch of the Fourth World Movement (ATD Cuarto Mundo, in
Spanish) followed a meeting in 1987 between Joseph Wresinski and Marco Aurelio Ugarte,
a Professor of Anthropology at San Antonio Abad National University in Cusco. The non-
governmental organization ATD Cuarto Mundo was formally founded in Cusco in
November 1991. The founding members were, from the beginning, close to the poor.

69. This chapter was originally prepared in Spanish by José Dimas Pérez Vanegas (Guatemala), María
Antonieta Pino de Navarrate, Yaque Gusmán Oviedo, Karely Paredes Ochoa, Marco Aurelio Ugarte
Ochoa, Nicolás Vladimiro Pino Amache, and Charles Sleeth (all from the Peru team), and María Julia
Pino Amache and Charo Carasco Cuba (Bolivia team). The paper was translated in English by Diego
Angel-Urdinola and edited for this report by Quentin Wodon and Jean-Marie Anglade. The views
expressed in this chapter are those of the authors, and they do not necessarily represent those of the World
Bank, its Executive Directors, or the countries they represent.

Families from rural and urban communities told the team that a better education and access to knowledge for their children was a priority for them. From the start, these were the projects the team focused on.

The Peru team works mainly in two geographic areas. The urban area of El Bosque is located in Southeast Cusco, about half way up one of the mountains surrounding the city. During the rainy season, a creek and several water sources overflow, so that many houses are damaged by the flood. The poorest families are usually the most harmed because they live in the most vulnerable areas. The Kuyo Grande Community is a peasant community in the Pisac District located one and a half hours from Cusco. The majority of the population speaks Quechua and works in agriculture and livestock-related activities. There is also a small group of artisans.

In El Bosque, adult members of the community thought initially that Cuarto Mundo was an NGO that would offer food and clothing. When we explained that our purpose was different, the neighbors did not pay much attention. Yet we were not discouraged. We approached the children through games. Eventually, a program for children and adults was developed in 1992 called "Useful Vacations." The program consisted of activities for children, such as crafting, reading, dances, and sports; and sowing and clothing design for youngsters and women.

In the Kuyo Gande Community, based on our experience in El Bosque, we thought about establishing a relationship with the children during school holidays. We soon realized, however, that we could not initiate actions directed only towards the children from the poorest families. Less poor families within the community, who have control over the community's life, would not allow it. As a result, upon the request of various families who were concerned about their children's performance at school, the association started in 1997 a holiday refresher course. Five young university students majoring in education, who were members of the Cuarto Mundo group, initiated this action. They would stay in the community five days a week and would come back to Cusco for the weekend. On Fridays, they would meet with two other members of the organization who were more experienced in order to evaluate weekly activities and reflect on them.

The community made classrooms from its school available for the activity. In each classroom, the student in charge would look after a group of 8 to 10 children organized by age groups. Based on their parent's wishes, the activities mainly included classes which focused on mathematics, languages, history, etc., but some time was also dedicated to other activities such as painting. The children who participated in these activities at the beginning were not members from the poorest families in the community. Yet, these children were very shy. Their attitudes changed as the coordinators started playing with them during break times. At the beginning children would stare at them, very surprised, but then they got used to it, giving space for a closer relationship.

During the school year, it was common for children to give gifts such as potatoes, corn, or beans to teachers. Children started to do the same with members of Cuarto Mundo, but the coordinators politely refused those gifts as they knew that many families were already giving much of what they had in order to provide their children with an education. Children would come back home worried, carrying back their gifts until one day a child came into the classroom with flowers for one of the coordinators. She accepted the gift with surprise and admiration. Seeing this, other children asked her if she liked flowers and she answered "yes." The following day, many children came to class with beautiful flowers and classrooms from then on were full of them. There were between 20 and 30 children in each classroom. During the school year, the news of the existence of this activity spread and in 1998 more children, this time from all the families of the community, joined the program.

In the following years, these vacation-learning activities continued to be carried in both El Bosque and in Kuyo Grande. In Kuyo Grande, the initial emphasis put on academic school support became eventually less important. Outdoor campgrounds replaced classrooms. In both places, activities were similar in the sense that they would allow children to discover their hidden and unknown talents through projects related to art, crafting, and theater. These activities were called "knowledge festivals," and would also include participation of people from all walks of life who were willing to share their knowledge with the children. This took place once a year.

Apart from this yearly event, "street" and rural libraries were also initiated. These had a different type of dynamic because they operated on a regular basis, usually during the weekends, all year long. The purpose of these outdoor libraries was to promote interactions among children without exclusion, always pursuing the participation of children from the poorest and most excluded families who often have the most limited access to knowledge.

On the streets or in rural areas, the libraries operate outdoor with books placed on the floor. This way, children who are shy participate because they do not need to knock at a door, or ask permission to join. The set up also allows parents to join the activity if they so wish. The street library coordinators select books according to the preferences of the children they expect to see. Books are always of very good quality and content, such as storybooks, books about animal life, art, geography, music, science, or any other topic that children like. Each library has an activity table set up so that children can paint or do any other manual work that they can be proud of. Before starting the libraries, the coordinators go from door to door to invite local children. This allows the coordinators to interact, get to know the parents, and better understand what they hope for their children. Both in the Kuyo Grande community and in the El Bosque neighborhood, the activities have taken place for several years now. In El Bosque, the place of the libraries changed several times to make the participation of children who didn't take part in the activities easier.

These activities allowed the team to get closer to families living in extreme poverty. However, reaching these families requires patience. Enabling them to regain their trust in others takes time. The first encounters usually involve rejection. The adults do not want to establish a conversation, and only answer what is merely necessary. However, they carefully observe our gestures and attitudes; the way we greet them, the way we shake hands with them and the way we accept some food they may offer to us. The recurrence of our visits and our concern about their children's future and their daily struggles progressively allow us to break the ice.

In Kuyo Grande, whenever we went to the home of one of the poorest families in the community, we used to notice another house, a little further, which seemed to be even more isolated. One day, we decided to go to this house and met Isabel, a 7-year-old girl who stared at us with curiosity. We took out a book, and invited her to read with us. She was very shy. Sitting close to the book, she would listen and look at the pictures. After that, she took the book, smiled, and started reading with us. A little later, from inside the house, her mother told Isabel to come back in. The lady barely looked at us and went back into the house.

Isabel's interest in reading a book made her come back to the place where we first met outside her home. We started a friendship through the books. We were continually wondering

---

Box 6.1: One Day in a Street Library in El Bosque

In one of the street libraries of El Bosque, we went to the small Saqramayo river that crosses the neighborhood. As we went there, we invited children to come after asking permission from their parents. Some children, when they saw us, started yelling at us from their homes so that we would wait for them and continue together. Fifteen children were present that day as we set up the books. Claudia and Luciano started fighting over a book of riddles. Mariela picked up two books to read to her younger siblings. Other children who didn't know how to read approached her. Mariela likes to be surrounded by other children and when she has some difficulty reading a word from the books, she goes to the coordinators for help. In the meantime, Luciano and Claudia solved their conflict by sharing the book. They tried to solve puzzles together and were encouraged by the coordinators to share with other children some of the riddles that they had solved.

After some time with the books, we left them under some trees and went to play with a ball. We formed teams of boys and girls. While we played, Juan, a youngster of 20 years of age who does not hang around with others due to his job as a ticket seller in the buses, came by and asked us for one of our storybooks. While we were still playing, some other children approached Juan in order to listen to what he was reading. After a while Juan left. Half an hour later, he came back with his spouse and two children. His forehead was sweating. He told us that he went to pick up his sons so that they could listen to the stories he was reading. Other children came closer, at the beginning not to listen to Juan but to get to know his children. Juan had picked a book with big pictures and little text. He would tell the story from the pictures. Although he had some difficulty reading, he wanted to share his imagination with his children and others. The street library over that weekend was very important for Juan and his family because for the fist time other children approached him without fear and with the intention to meet his family.

why Isabel would always be home and would not go to school. One day she told us that her teacher told her that she was dumb because she did not know how to read. Then we understood why she liked books so much. Every time we met Isabel, the attitude of her mother, Mrs. Marcela, was similar; she would be ice-cold, hide her face, and barely acknowledge us. She would not talk to anybody, but with her neighbor who also happened to be her cousin. Even after a full year, Mrs. Marcela would still not talk to us. We did not know what to do to change this. We felt frustrated, incapable of gaining this new family's trust. Yet one day, as we were reading, Mrs. Marcela came out; she came closer to us and shook our hand. We realized that her face had several scars probably due to burns, which could have been the reason why she would not to come and greet us. She stayed with us looking at the pictures and listening to the stories. We told her that Isabel liked books very much, and she explained to us why Isabel would not go to school.

In the street library that we set up in El Bosque, Pedro and Alberto, two brothers, would always hit each other. They would tease other children and therefore would create a bad environment for the rest of the group. Their family would often move due to conflicts with neighbors. Their father, Mr. Antonio, did not want his sons to participate in the street libraries. Aware of the conflicts he had in the community, he did not want other children to harm or humiliate them.

For nine months, the family left the neighborhood and we did not see Pedro and Alberto anymore. After some time, the family came back to El Bosque. When we were running the street library, the youngest child would stare at us from afar, but as we invited them to join, they did not want to get together with the other children. As time passed by, Pedro turned into a young adolescent and would help us with the library. He would often ask us for books to take home. This made us realize that we could go to his home and read with his younger siblings and start a relationship with them. The first time we went to visit them at home, we proposed to three other children from the community to come with us. They seemed rather unsure about going along with us but Pedro's mother, Mrs. Cristina, kindly received us. She asked us about what we wanted, and we answered that we were bringing some books and wanted to share them with her younger children. She sat down on the floor, called her children and told them: "They brought books for you, come along and behave well."

A few months later, children from the neighborhood wanted to return with us to Mrs. Cristina's house. As we approached her house, some of them felt again a little unsure but nevertheless came along. As we were reading a book to one of the children, Mrs. Cristina started to laugh loudly. We saw her acting as a young girl, but the other children felt uncomfortable about it and started to leave one by one. At the end, we were the only ones in the house, together with Mrs. Cristina and her children. Later, Mr. Antonio, the father, came into the house. He was acting in a strange way. He did not even look at us, and went into his room without saying a word. Mrs. Cristina stopped laughing immediately. She became nervous and went to her husband's room. Her children left the books on the floor and also left the room. We thought somebody would come out and bode us farewell, but nobody came and we decided to leave the house. Neighbors asked us about what happened, and whether we had been thrown out of the house. We answered that we had just finished reading the books. As we were leaving, the neighbor told us that somebody was calling us. We turned and saw Mr. Antonio who was waving good-bye to us. This gesture gave us the confidence we needed to come back another day.

Families trapped in poverty live in a very closed world. The street libraries take place in their community because it is their first place of reference. Yet, the families have also the right to widen their horizon and discover what happens beyond their neighborhood and hometown. The books used in the street library are a way to widen their world. Among the activities of the Peruvian association, we tried to create other opportunities that allow children to broaden their horizon and develop different aspects of their personality. Here are two examples.

A first example is related to a literary contest called "Working Children" organized by CODENI NGO (Coordinadora de los Derechos del Niño). Juan Carlos was living in El Bosque and was 12 years old at the time. He was a shoe polisher and decided to participate in this contest by telling others his own life story. He asked one of the coordinators of the street library to help him write the text and send it to the contest. Two months later, he heard on the radio on the streets of Cusco that CODENI was looking for him in order to award him the first prize - a bicycle. This bicycle was the first one in El Bosque, and Juan Carlos would lend it in turns to his friends. Years later, a group of youngsters in El Bosque were looking for a story to put together a play. Juan Carlos offered his story, but the group made fun of it. Juan Carlos approached one of the members of the association and asked to please give the story back to him. "They don't understand it yet", he said, "When they do, they won't make fun of it and I will give it back to them." What impressed us was to see the importance the story had for Juan Carlos, and at the same time, the understanding he showed towards the reactions of the group.

A second example relates to events which are organized every October 17th, the international day for the eradication of poverty. In Cusco, there is an exhibition featuring the work done by the children who participated in the street libraries. In 1999, a delegation of children from Kuyo Grande was gathered to participate in the exhibition. Some members of the association thought that Marcos, a very shy boy who did not participate much in the street library, could be part of the delegation. When we went to visit Marco's father, we took some of Marcos' drawings. His father was surprised to see his son's work and told us with pride: "Yes, my son can come with you; I see he is very smart and think he will be a good delegate." Marcos was part of the delegation from Kuyo Grande for two years. Each time he was confident in explaining his work and the work of others. The coordinators realized that Marcos became more involved in the libraries. In 2002, he was elected treasurer of his school and he has been very responsible about his duties ever since.

To conclude this section, it is worth spelling out some of the criteria that serve as guidelines when, within the Cuarto Mundo association, we evaluate our actions and their impacts. The most important criterion is the participation of the poorest. Are children and families who participate in the activities the ones who should benefit the most from them, that is, the most isolated? If not, what is the reason for their absence?

One of the strongest wishes parents have is that their children be given access to knowledge. Part of the evaluation process then consists of clarifying whether or not this is the case among the poorest children. When Mrs. Jesusa, a very poor mother from Kuyo Grande, saw her children's drawings from the street libraries, she was very surprised. She said that her children had never been to school, and that she did not know they could draw. She thought her children did not have the ability to study and this in addition to lack of money, was a key reason why she would not sent them to school. She did not want her children to be embarrassed because they could appear to be dumb. After seeing what her children were capable of, Mrs. Jesusa and her husband were highly motivated to spend an enormous amount of effort to enroll their children in school, pay the fees, and buy school supplies. Nowadays, their children's education is a family priority. But success is not always achieved at first. In another family of Kuyo Grande one girl was enrolled in school after participating in the rural libraries, but dropped out the following year. Whether the outcome is negative or positive, such information must be compiled in order to guide and modify future actions.

We also learned that it is important to consider other questions in the evaluation of the activities, such as: "Did the activities lead the children to be more confident about themselves and more aware of their capabilities?" and "Did the activities allow the poorest children to build a better relationship with other children in the community?" Children who feel rejected or excluded cannot take full advantage of school and some of them end up dropping out. We have seen before how Marcos became more confident and how he became a representative of his class as he gained confidence in himself. These outcomes are sometimes difficult to spot, but are important in an evaluation process.

When evaluating the outcomes of the actions taken, one must try to take into account all the impacts that such actions may have on the poorest families, both at the personal as well as at the institutional level. For example, a student majoring in education who participated in the coordination of the street libraries learned that the parents of the poorest families wanted their children to learn and go to school whereas before she thought otherwise. This reflected an evolution in her thinking and it was an important realization for a student who would become a teacher. By contrast, if we see that after a long interaction with a school the poorest children are still isolated and excluded, and are not treated like the other children, such an outcome would have to be analyzed more closely in order to achieve a more positive result in future endeavors.

The evaluation of an action taken involves knowing what the poorest families think about such an action. At times they express their visions with words, at other times with their silence, and sometimes with gestures or attitudes of approval or disapproval. The evaluation is a process that needs time and closeness to the poorest families and to the community in which they live.

Whilst the founding members of Cuarto Mundo Peru chose to support very poor parents for the education of their children, they also wanted the families who are the poorest and the most excluded to be recognized by society. In order to do so, we tried to involve different institutions in our actions, including the San Antonio de Abad University. As a result of the partnership with the university, a library, the " Joseph Wresinski Library: Extreme Poverty and Human Rights," was established. Its purpose was to open the university's doors to the poorest. After a long dialog, the municipality of Cusco also allowed delegates from the most excluded families to honor the flag of Tahuantinsuyo, which is an important Andean Region symbol located in the main square of the city. Usually, such honor is exclusively reserved for important institutional authorities. Many poor families saw in such a gesture the recognition of their struggle and strength.

Understanding the Life of Poor Children and their Parents: Doña Elena's Family in Guatemala

The Cuarto Mundo group in Guatemala was founded in 1978, when Joseph Wresinski sent staff to work with Caritas, a small group of committed women within the Catholic Church that had worked in Guatemala since 1965. The Cuarto Mundo team went to the San Jacinto municipality in the department of Chiquimila, in the eastern part of the country. The original objectives set by the team were to learn about the region and its population, particularly about the poor and their situation within their communities; it was also to take the time necessary to assimilate the society's thoughts, wishes, and goals in a manner which would respect the society's members. The activities focused on promoting health, nutrition, and access to knowledge. The time spent with the families in Chiquimula was used to learn about the realities of a multicultural country. The team learned about the patience and wisdom of a people who suffered from conflict. The knowledge and experience gained in Chiquimula was useful later for team members working in other locations. Members of the team moved to Guatemala City in 1987 to implement a program promoting access to culture and knowledge in poor neighborhoods. In 1988, activities were started along the area of the capital's trash disposal and besides the railroads, near the bus terminal and the city's great market. In 1991, team members moved to Honduras, to the Nueva Suyapa neighborhood, a poor area in Tegucigalpa, the nation's capital.

Doña Elena has had a long story with the Guatemala association, which started in 1988 at the site of the railway in Guatemala city. She told us:

> I was around 10 years old when I first came to live by the railway with my mom. We came from the south of Guatemala. At the beginning the place was a trash disposal area, and police would often evict us, but we would build our house again. We managed not to be thrown out. When we first came, our first covacha was not even a *covacha* (a *covacha* is a very poor dwelling). It was simply a bunch of plastic, just like a doll house. We were very poor and that is why we lived by the railway. My mom would go to the area where trucks are unloaded in order to pick up beans and corn from the floor.

In 1995, along with another 1084 families who lived by the railway, Doña Elena moved to a location in the city's suburbs. She had put in this project a great deal of hope because she would finally own a piece of land in a place where her children would be safe from the dangers of the trains. However a few months later Doña Elena was one of the first to move out from this new neighborhood because, as she would explain, "over there, my children were starving." Together with her seven children and her spouse, Don Alex, she returned to the railroad, close to the terminal's market, because it was easier to find work and food there. She had to move to a very remote place, one which would give a terrible sense of isolation. Her situation was even worse than before when she first left the railroad.

To make a living, Don Alex collected old metal parts, glass, aluminum, and boxes. One would always see him walking down the streets and sometimes his children would come along with him. The children would run down the street and as they would find a useful object, they would show it to him: "Dad, look at what I have found!" He would answer, It is good, put it in the bag" or "It's useless." In so doing, he would share with them what he knew.

The family did not have chairs or tables inside their house. At times, the children had only radish with salt for breakfast. When a member of the team went into their house to invite the children for a street library, he saw Doña Elena taking off the buttons from a dirty shirt and putting them on her daughter Maritza's only clean dress so that she could go to the activity. She could not wash their clothes because she did not have soap.

One day Pablo, the 9-year-old son of Doña Elena, did not return home from school. His mother looked desperately for him. She even left her job because of it. She went to various places to ask about him, but nobody knew where he was. She was desperate and could barely sleep. Then she came to the Cuarto Mundo team to ask us if we could go with her to a center that welcomes children from the street. We went to the center, and when we asked for Pablo, they told us that they had not seen him. They suggested that we go to another center from the same institution to check if he was there instead. When we arrived at that center, we were told that Pablo was not there, but at that very moment, he appeared at the door. His sister Maritza shouted, "Pablo, there he is!" Doña Elena asked, "Son, you are o.k.? I have looked for you a great deal." They embraced and Doña Elena cried. A great deal of happiness was showing on their faces. Doña Elena asked him if he wanted to come back home and he said yes.

The person in charge of the center explained that they were picking up children who were on the streets. They take those who appear to be in danger, or who could fall for drugs, and they try to save them before something bad happens. Doña Elena tried to explain that her son was clean of vice, that he left to play with other boys one day and did not return. She said, "I have other children and I am alone. I have to work to get them some food. Therefore they remain alone at home, but I work to get us food. I have been without work for a month looking for him."

On the way back home, Doña Elena said:

> This morning, before leaving, I asked God to put me on the right track to find my son. He listened to me. Ever since the time I left home, I felt that I was going to find him today... Before I did not feel well. I felt awkward when he was not there. Now I do not know what happened to me. I cannot believe it. He is with me. I have spent days and nights lost in thoughts. Before, when we ate, I did not feel well.

She continued to speak to Pablo and Maritza: "I want you to be with me. I love you a great deal. I want to have you by my side, so that we will always be together. I was in pain". Pablo then said, "I thought that you were not looking for me, because others told me so."

In 1999, the last families who still lived by the railway were moved to a different place, a 45 minutes driving distance away from the Terminal's market. Doña Elena was one of them. Many families were happy to go to a safer place. But, at the same time, they felt sad to see that this place, where some had lived for 20 to 30 years, would be destroyed without leaving any trace of their lives there. The fact is that in many countries, the right to make and tell history, is a right frequently denied to the very poor. Only on a few occasions do children have the opportunity to know about the struggles and achievements of their elders and parents. This was the starting point of a two-year project with the objective to create, with the poorest families who lived along the Railroad track, an exhibition to collect their voices and their images, so that they could preserve a page of their history.

For Doña Elena, who was now alone after the death of her spouse (who had been hit by a truck), this second departure from the railroad track required a new process of adaptation to a community that was not moving at the pace of the poor. She would have to deal with

---

Box 6.2: Gerson

When confidence and trust have been built, one can have access to information about the life of families who live in extreme poverty that would not have been available otherwise. When people have suffered for years from social exclusion, they know that it is more prudent for them to be silent. But when they are certain that what they are going to say is not going to be used against them, their words can be very powerful. The following was written by Gerson, the second son of Doña Elena, when he was 17 years old. He wrote it in 1999, for the celebration of the 17th of October, the United Nations' International Day for the Eradication of Poverty.

> I was born by the railroad; I lived there all my childhood and part of my youth. We, the children of the railroad, were happy; our parents were always close to us. At times they would leave us locked in the house because they were afraid of the train and of the thieves. If we were in the street, our mothers would come to see us occasionally to see if we were o.k. and to check with whom we were. When we were children, we used to play all together. With the help of the street libraries, we were able to open our minds and spend time with and be close to good people who were interested in us. At the Railroad, we learned many things, some good and others we would have been better off without; but above all, we learned from our parents. The majority of our parents worked at the Terminal, as carriers, salespersons, and also washing other people's clothes. Thanks to their effort, we could go to school. They always tried to make our life simpler than the one they had to live. Therefore they did their utmost to give us an education. When our parents needed help in difficult times, we would also begin to work and support the family. If our childhood was good, it was, above all, because of the support from our parents. But also speaking for the children that we were and for the youngster that we are now, we thank those who treated us like persons and did not consider us a danger; among them, we thank Mrs. Sarita (who was a member of an Evangelical church and a close friend of the family of Doña Elena) and Cuarto Mundo because they were always supporting us.

Those are simple words, but if we take them seriously, as we must do, they challenge our understanding. Why does Gerson says: "We, the children of the Railroad, we were happy" when one knows the conditions in which people lived in that place? What does he mean when he says: "above all, we learned from our parents"? Listening to Gerson drives us to build with him and his family a new and better understanding of what the very poor live and think.

requests to participate in projects related to the infrastructure of the neighborhood, such as water, power, schools, hospital, or clinics, while her first priority was still to feed her children. Nowadays, Doña Elena still lives in that neighborhood.

Making sure that the actions which are carried with regard to what the poor and very poor people really think and hope is an ongoing challenge. Sometimes, an action derives directly from a simple observation. For example Marcos and Luis were two boys who participated regularly in the street library that was set up in front of the main trash disposal area in Guatemala City. One day, they told us that they did not find books that they liked. Marcos liked planes and Luis was fond of snakes. We looked for books on these topics and brought them to the following street library. On another occasion, the coordinators realized that a girl from a very poor family of the locality did not participate in the activities. When her mother would go to the trash disposal area to collect useful things, she would stay at her grand mother's place, who did not allow her to go outside the home. The library, then, was moved to where the child's grandmother lived so that she would let her participate in the activity.

At times, more time is needed to be sure of what a child or an adult really thinks. For several months for example, the members of the team wondered what Don Alex thought about the street library. When he and Doña Elena returned to live by the railroad, they ended up in a remote area, and the location of the street library was changed to be in front of their house. We placed the books for reading on a plastic sheet on the floor. Don Alex, when he was around, did not speak much. He would barely greet us and did not answer when we asked him for advice regarding the library. Yet one day, he came with a great orange plastic sheet that he had found on the street, and said: "When I saw it, I thought about you and I thought that it would be of great service to you in placing it on the floor, when the children read the books." On that day the team realized that Don Alex was really supporting the activities for the children, even if he had never actually said so. Before, we could only suspect it, but we could not be certain.

The hope that their children be given a chance to learn and have access to knowledge to get a better life than theirs is one of the very fundamental aspirations of very poor parents. Don Alex showed it through this orange plastic sheet. Doña Elena showed it often too, for example with Maritza, one of her daughters. After much effort, Doña Elena managed to enroll her in a school. Maritza began with a great deal of enthusiasm that school year. When she would go to the street library, the coordinators would ask her if she was attending the school, and she would respond positively. Even her teacher told the coordinators that Maritza was doing very well and that she had passed all her exams before Holy Week. But some weeks later, Doña Elena came to tell us that her daughter had been expelled from the school. Doña Elena could not believe it. She said,

> The director perhaps does not have children. I leave at 5 o'clock in the morning for work. If I do not work, who is going to bring food home? When I do not work, I have to sell my things, dresses, umbrella, apron, because the children have to eat. I tell the children that their best gift to us would be to do well at school. I insist every day that they go to school, but I do not know what to do; I am not able to manage them. I want them to learn because it is for their benefit.

On that day, Doña Elena asked a member of the team to speak to the director. The director accepted that Maritza would return to the school on the condition that if she were to miss classes for one single day, she would be expelled for good. This was a very difficult condition to comply with for Doña Elena and Maritza. A member of the team committed to go each morning, for the remainder of the school year, to pick up Maritza so that she would go to school. And so it happened; but without Doña Elena's strong desire to provide an education for her children, the team would probably not have taken the decision to escort Maritza to school each day.

Learning from the very poor families what their hopes are drives us to share them with other people outside the association. During the street libraries for example children and adults always enjoyed very much the presence of artists. From this experience, the project "Art For All" was born. With support from other organizations, hundreds of artists came to share their passion for art with the children and their families. In a dance class, Julia, the older daughter of Doña Elena, surprised all when she got up spontaneously and started to dance. It was often hard for her to be with the other children, as she would be rejected and harsh words about her and her family would be heard. Therefore, that day was a moment of great emotion to see her dancing and to see other children and some parents clapping at the rhythm of the music and shouting, "Julia, Julia." She lived through this moment with a great deal of pride.

We also tried to find other organizations which would enable children to pursue their education thanks to scholarships. In 2001, a hundred or so children that participated in the street libraries took advantage of scholarships provided by six such organizations. The collaboration was not always easy. At times, the organizations would set standards (such as requesting attendance in parent's meetings, or expecting excellence in the performance of the children) that were difficult to comply with for very poor families. Yet, through dialog, these difficulties were overcome most of the time.

When team members establish such contacts with other institutions, they must first explain what sort of life the poorest families endure, and that it takes time to understand their hopes little by little. They often think they have been heard and understood, but this is not always the case. Yet through both failures and successes, we are conscious that dialog with others is the path that should always be taken to let the world know about the life and hopes of the poorest families, so that their life may ultimately change.

Enabling Children to Learn from Each Other: The Tapori Network in Bolivia

Javier Espíndola met a member of the Movement when he was studying at the School of Public Health in Rennes, France. After he returned to his home country, Bolivia, he kept contact with ATD Fourth World. In 1988 he initiated, with friends, a group that would promote the ideas and work of Joseph Wresinski. Out of this group, an association of the Bolivian friends of the Cuarto Mundo was born and in 1996 two Swiss members of the Movement settled in the capital city of La Paz.

Their first objective was to learn about the people and the associations that were already involved in the fight against poverty, and to share with them their experience. They learned for example about the "Solidarity Team" in the city of El Alto near La Paz who monitors and gives support to poor families. They also learned about the work of the "Educational Teams," which are groups of teachers from public and private schools who get together to reflect on the education needs of the poor. It's thanks to the Educational Teams that the Tapori network was established in Bolivia.

Tapori is a movement based on friendship among children of all origins around the world. The objective is to create a movement among children, youngsters, and adults that promotes friendship and solidarity as instruments to fight poverty. A Tapori Letter is sent every two months to children and other people who would like to receive it. The letter contains news about children throughout the world who share their accomplishments, their sadness, and their dreams. It is a thought provoking document which encourages very concrete gestures of solidarity. The Tapori network has also published mini-books that tell real stories about children of the world who try to reject exclusion where they live. The Tapori movement has an international headquarter that promotes, every year, campaigns on topics of interest to children, with the objective to collect their thoughts and feelings, and disseminate them. In 2001 for example, a campaign on "Building Machines to Change the Way People Look" was launched.

The Tapori dynamic began in the schools of La Paz in 1998 when the members of the Bolivian Association invited several schools from the city to participate in a campaign called "Put a Feather and the Bird of Hope Will Fly." More than 1,000 feathers with children's messages were received. Little by little some teachers got acquainted with and involved in the Tapori dynamic. An interesting feature about mobilizing the teachers was that each one of them implemented Tapori differently, depending on their situation, adapting it to the children with whom they worked, as seen from the examples of María Luisa, Lourdes, Mercedes and Gema.

- María Luisa works in a zone of La Paz, considered to be a red zone, due to the violence existing over there. She used to say:

  > what is interesting to me about Tapori is its message of peace. I have brought Tapori to my students so that they can learn different realities, different experiences, so that they could reflect about friendship and solidarity by means of concrete gestures; I believe I have somehow accomplished that.

- Lourdes' school is located at the periphery of La Paz, a zone where many poor families live.

  > When I shared with my students texts about Joseph Wresinski's childhood, I realized that many of them could identify with it and that was very important for them. I did not really know the life of my students; it helped me to go beyond what I thought about their life and the life of their families…. This year I have four new children coming from other centers and I did not have the time to introduce them to the other children. But when I entered the classroom, the children had already welcomed them. I asked the students if they knew the names of the new children, and they did. Before, teachers were the ones who introduced new children. Now children are the ones to do so. I feel that I am raising respect among men and women.

- Mercedes is the director and promoter of a school and of a dining room in a low-middle class neighborhood, where children have few options for entertainment. She saw in Tapori an alternative,

  > In this area, there are no country clubs, movie theaters, or parks where the youth can get together; so the children started to organize many activities some of which were not positive. Tapori is an alternative that gives them a space for thought and offers them the opportunity to share their views with each other…. With Tapori I succeeded in having parents communicating with their children. In this type of neighborhoods, parents feel a lot of pressure and they often cannot spend time with their children. Tapori gives an opportunity to parents and children to communicate with each other.

■ Gema is a teacher in a private school located in one of the most privileged zones of the city. She said,

> Tapori is important to me because it allows my students, who come from well-to-do families, to get to know poor children; not only through gestures of charity, but also through gestures of friendship and fraternity.

The Tapori movement is supported by a great deal of commitment from teachers, but other members of the community are also involved. Marcela is a business administrator who supports a Tapori secretariat in the Andean Region. She explains how she got involved in the movement:

> In 1998, members of the Association invited me to travel to the region of Potosí in order to reach out to some children. It came to my mind that we had to carry something (clothes, food, etc.) but they told me not to; and that instead we would carry a Tapori suitcase. I said: "Are you aware of the level of misery in that place!" I was very nervous to go to visit poor children without giving them anything, and I departed a little frustrated. But when we arrived they said, "You have not brought us anything, that's fine. When people bring things there is always conflict here because there is never enough for all." There, I realized that I could share other things with them: friendship, attention. I realized that it is possible to help the poor without giving material things to them. From that moment on, I became committed to the poorest children and families.

For several years, Marcela, together with other members, encouraged the practice of Tapori in another neighborhood in La Paz. The group of San Marcos in La Paz was started as

---

Box 6.3: Tapori Activities in Lourdes' and Gema's Schools

Lourdes: "Together with the children and their parents, I worked on a show based on Joseph Wresinski's life story. The children became very motivated after I told them his story; so I proposed to them to draw, with the help of their parents, a picture reflecting a certain part of the story. I prepared a television set made of cardboard in which we placed the sheets of paper, one after the other, sequentially. We presented the show on the last day of school. The children invited their parents. A girl told the story using the drawings; this was then followed by a discussion. Many children and parents were moved by the story and some shared some of their own stories. The following are comments made by three of the participants: 'My dad too sometimes does not come home when he does not find a job; some times he comes home mad'; 'I am from east Bolivia; I have come here, where I do not know anybody, in search for an opportunity for me and for my daughter'; 'I wake up every day to look for a job, but everyday is the same, and that does not allow me to be relaxed.'"

Gema: "There were four children in the classroom, and they were very quiet because they did not come from the same social background. As more children arrived, we encouraged them to participate in a game about friendship; but this game only involves four players and there were more than nine children. Some said, 'I want to go first!' We told them that they could play in groups. This way, nobody would be alone or excluded from the game. Other children arrived and the ones already playing invited them to join their groups; they laughed, sung, and shouted. Nobody was quiet any longer. At the end, we asked the children what they had learned and what they enjoyed about the game. Luciano got up and said 'It pleased me a great deal when in the game one of the instructions was that we had to wait for the groups that were last so that there was not a single winning group; we all won together.' Veronica said: 'Without friendship one cannot be happy.' Eduardo said: 'If all of us united no matter our differences in being poor or rich, the world would be different too.'"

a result of Marcela's initiative with help from other members of the Bolivian Association. Initially, they invited their own children and other friends from their neighborhood. Now, encouraged by their teachers, more children have joined. At present, there are 30 children in the group between 8 and 15 years of age. They meet two times a month, every other Saturday in the afternoon. Another group exists in the municipality of Coroico. There, children meet around laundries which were built so that all the families in the community, especially the poorest, could have access to them. This group is lead by three persons and meets every other Saturday.

What brings together children of different social background is their desire to share and be children of the world. Children know that friendship and gestures of solidarity are important to bring about change and that they should have the opportunity to put this knowledge in practice. The following examples show how children found such an opportunity in Tapori activities:

■ To commemorate the 17th of October, children and their teachers were invited to participate in a Tapori exhibition of drawings and messages. A few days before Gema said: "I have invited the children of my school, but I do not believe they will participate. I do not believe that their parents would like to bring them. Maybe 2 or 3 will come." The first day of the exhibition, various children from poor neighborhoods including those who came to the street libraries were present. Gema was very surprised when she saw that many children from her class had arranged to share a music display. They brought their instruments, including a piano, and they encouraged other children to sing and to participate in the display. Gema said:

> I did not force the children to come. They came out of their own will. I cannot believe it! Also, I am very happy because some months ago, they would have probably brought candy to give away to poor children. But this time they came to share their own music.

■ Wendy, who for many years had been familiar with Tapori activities, said:

> I learned about Tapori in 1998 through a school teacher, when I was 9 years old. I discovered there that all human beings, whether they are rich, poor, black, or white, should have the same opportunities and rights, and that our opinions have great value. I learned to listen to the problems faced by the poorest children and realized that the most important thing is the friendship that unites us. When one is alone, one feels sad, but when one has friends, one feels good. Tapori made me dream and hope that some day the world would change, and that change would come when adults change their ways of thinking and acting. Now, I am the one who has to teach children what I have learned. They should discover and learn about friendship, and about sharing with children who are excluded.

Teachers who help in the Tapori movement are of the opinion that this kind of dynamic improves the work and values that are taught in their schools. The teachers are the first to change as Lourdes explained it:

> Before Tapori, I did not think that getting to know my students' life was a priority. Now I think it is very important because I can identify why they have such difficulties. Tapori has changed my life and nowadays I feel closer to them. Now I think about how their families live.

Now I can become a friend of the children. I do whatever is possible, so parents can see me also as a friend and they can trust me as well. With this, I learned that I have to spend time visiting my students' home, because many parents still feel that they are going to be alienated at school. I would like to share more with them.

A change in the mentality and behavior are signals that a community is looking at the poorest in a different way. Organizations and institutions may begin to change as well, as illustrated by examples from two schools in poor neighborhoods in the city of Alto. A team member explained:

We organized, with the collaboration of teachers from two schools, a "Festival of Knowledge—Art and Culture." The children and teachers suggested that all present something, like a drawing, poetry, or dancing. They invited children from various classes to participate and learn about the activities. At the end of the show, every student presented his or her work and received a diploma. The purpose of this festival was not to create an environment where some children win and others loose. The purpose was to give the opportunity to students to participate, so they could teach and share with one another. At the end of the festival, a teacher said: "This was a forum to encourage all children to participate. Sometimes as teachers, we never take a look at the poorest children. We focus on the best. Not only do I have to know all my students and their families, but I also have to give them the opportunity they deserve here at school."

Box 6.4: Juanita (By a Member of the ATD Fourth World Bolivian Team)

Juanita is 9 years old. She has three older brothers: Esteban, Marcos, and Pedro. They live with their mother, Mrs. Claudia who suffers from arthritis and can barely move. Esteban, Marcos, and Pedro study thanks to their work as "voceadores" (Bus announcers) and the support of "The Solidarity Team of El Alto." What they earn at work is just enough to pay for transportation and food. Juanita studies at the neighborhood school. When I go to see her, I never know whether I will find her sad or happy. It all depends on how it goes at school and with the people of the neighborhood. Sometimes some boy would hit her while playing in the park. Other times, children at school say things to her regarding her sick mother, and she feels humiliated when her teacher confronts her in front of her classmates when she has not done her homework or when she lacks some material. The teacher asks her to bring her parents to school; but Mrs. Claudia cannot walk. Then, the teacher punishes Juanita and at times insults her and her family.

Yet when Juanita talks about her school, she does it with a great deal of happiness. She does her homework while singing songs, and Mrs. Claudia is always telling how wonderful Juanita is. After that, Juanita's face shines. On the 17th of October of the year 2001, we organized a knowledge Festival in Juanita's school. This was a good opportunity to learn about her life in the school. On that day, Juanita's teacher was preparing some drawings with Juanita's classmates, but Juanita did not want to approach them. She stayed with me holding my hand. I went to the place where her teacher was. When the teacher saw Juanita, she took her by her jacket and guided her to a seat. Later, addressing the other children, she said that nobody should be like her. All the children remained silent and Juanita no longer had the opportunity to continue her drawing.

One often does not realize the damage that can be done to children living in poverty, the suffering and struggle that they face every day. It is important to know their life. It is not enough to simply judge them based on their appearance. If one cannot change the manner in which the world often looks at children such as Juanita and at their families, nothing will change in their lives. The Tapori movement's aim is to contribute to bringing about that change.

Conclusion

The ATD Fourth World's teams in Peru, Guatemala, and Bolivia shared experiences from the daily life of very poor families: a mother who goes to work very early in the morning so that her children can eat; another mother who encourages her daughter to keep working at school even though she is having a difficult time there; a father who teaches to his children what he knows so that they can earn a living in the future; parents who do as much as they can so that their children may learn.

Much of what the very poor do to survive is unknown to outsiders. Without the support that they give to each other, their life would be unbearable. It is often said that development programs do not reach the poorest. If these programs do not manage to take into account and build upon the daily acts of resistance from these families, they will indeed not change the lives of these families because they will remain alien to their strengths and hopes. Yet, to recognize these daily efforts and build upon them, time, proximity, and true commitment are needed. Flexibility is required as well. The Guatemala team always considered that Doña Elena's family suffered from a particularly strong level of social exclusion and the team maintained a strong relationship with her. That is why, every time that Doña Elena had to move, alone or with other families, the team would move the street library close to where she would be. By doing so, they would also discover new places where the very poor people live.

The Peru team explained how Mrs. Jesusa and her husband enrolled their children into school. This was their victory. It was not achieved through a poster or a campaign. It resulted from their relationship with a group of people who decided to bring books and read them to their children, so that they realized that their children did have the ability to learn and that they could make it through school. The Guatemala team told how Doña Elena began searching for her son after he did not come back home. She started the search alone, even if it meant leaving her job. But at some point, she needed and sought the help of other people to pursue what she had already begun. The Bolivia team explained how difficult it is to change the way through which the world looks at the poorest families. Yet, it can be done, provided committed people are set about to change these views. This commitment must be maintained over time. More than one year of regular visits by the Peru team were necessary for Mrs. Marcela to begin a conversation with the team members who came to read books with her daughter. In Guatemala, time was also needed to ascertain that Don Alex was supportive of the street library in which his children were participating.

Many times, the poorest families have seen people coming to their neighborhood to carry out a project that lasts for some days, weeks or months, and then the people are gone without setting up something that could bring about a significant improvement in the lives of these families. Before giving their trust, the poor will make sure that the people with whom they are dealing are ready to be loyal to them. Only through time and regular contacts can one build this trust. A key lesson then from this chapter is that if development programs are to reach the very poor, they must consider these very poor families as the first and main protagonist of the fight against poverty. They must also emphasize the importance of a long-term commitment to support poor families in their daily endeavors.

PART III

Experiences from Developed Countries

CHAPTER 7

The Story of the "Unleashing Hidden Potential" Seminar in the United States

Carl Egner[70]

This chapter tells the story of a seminar which took place in November 2000 on unleashing the hidden potential of very poor children in the United States. In underprivileged schools, parents and teachers alike are under a great deal of pressure. What too often results is that everyone tries to find someone else to blame. Parents hope desperately that their children will not repeat their own school failures, and when they see their children struggling in school they often lash out at the teachers. Teachers are often ill-prepared to deal with conditions they find in high poverty schools, and teachers in these schools are often less trained and less experienced than teachers in other schools. In these circumstances, teachers can accuse the parents of their students of being bad parents, of not even caring about their children's education. In the face of these conflicting accusations the ones who suffer most are the children. Yet the Unleashing Hidden Potential seminar showed that it is possible for people from very different backgrounds and very different perspectives to put aside their differences and seriously try to work together for the benefit of children.

One time when a shooting happened at Corey's school, I said, "You're not going back to school over there. You're just going to stay home. Either let them place you in another school or you're going to stay home with me." Corey looked up and said, "No, I'm not. I do have to go to school and get my education. I am willing to die for my education. I'm not worrying about them boys. That's on them. They're fighting." In other words, he is saying, "Just because this occurred in the school is no reason for me to stop going to school. You may be scared, but I'm not scared. I'm just going there for one thing and one thing only—to get an education."

---

70. Carl Egner is a member of the USA Fourth World team.

In the United States, education is consistently ranked as one of the more important concerns of citizens. Education is a prominent topic in most elections, both national and local. The newspapers contain frequent articles about public schools, often highlighting the shortcomings of the U.S. educational system, or, on the other hand, describing a new educational initiative that seems to hold promise for solving some of the system's seemingly intractable problems. Educational improvement is also the topic of extensive research among academics and policymakers.

Within all this talk and research about education, one of the areas that has received considerable attention is that of parental involvement. There is evidence that parental involvement in schooling has a positive impact on student achievement. One study, for example, examined over 50 different studies on parental involvement and concluded, "Taken as a whole, these studies found a positive and convincing relationship between family involvement and benefits for students, including academic achievement. This relationship holds across families of all economic, racial/ethnic, and educational backgrounds and for students of all ages."[71]

U.S. national law also recognizes the importance of parent involvement. The No Child Left Behind Act of 2001 requires, for example, that all schools receiving federal educational support funds are required to develop a parental involvement policy, and that parents are expected to be involved in the development of this policy. The law also speaks of the "shared responsibility" of both parents and educators for improving student achievement.[72]

There are also numerous organizations around the country that aim to facilitate, in a wide variety of ways, parent involvement in public schools. These range from organizations like the National PTA (Parent Teachers Association) that operate largely within the framework of the school system, to organizations like ACORN (Association of Community Organizations for Reform Now) that operate outside of the formal educational structure and try to bring change through community and political organizing.

Despite all these efforts, however, there can be confusion about what exactly is meant by "parental involvement." Among teachers, for example, some, often in middle-class schools, complain that parents are *too* involved, meaning that the teachers feel that some parents are meddling in details of school life that should best be left to professional educators. Other teachers, often in lower-income schools, complain that parents are *not enough* involved, meaning that the teachers feel that parents should for example be more involved in checking children's homework or at least ensuring that homework is actually completed.

Parental involvement can mean very different things to different people. Parents themselves are also obviously not all alike; they can have different ideas about how they want to be involved in their children's education or very different possibilities for how they can be involved.

This article is about the educational involvement of parents who live in persistent poverty. There is a special set of challenges involved in building positive relationships between

---

71. Anne T. Henderson and Karen L. Mapp, *A New Wave of Evidence: The Impact of School, Family, and Community Connections on Student Achievement,* (Austin, TX: National Center for Family & Community Connections with Schools, Southwest Educational Development Laboratory, 2002) p. 24. Full document available at: www.sedl.org/connections/resources/evidence.pdf.

72. United States Congress. "No Child Left Behind Act of 2001." (Washington, DC: United States Congress, 2002). Full text of the law available at: www.ed.gov/policy/elsec/leg/esea02/107-110.pdf. The examples cited here are contained in Section 1118, Subsection b, Part 1 and in Section 1118, Subsection d.

these parents and the schools their children attend. Often parents living in poverty do not have positive memories of their own time in school, and so they feel reluctant to put themselves into a situation where they might be criticized. Teachers in low-income, inner city schools are also often under a great deal of pressure. Many teachers at these schools are new to the profession and have not been adequately prepared for what they find once they are put in charge of a classroom of children. In these situations, taking time to build positive relations with parents can seem like a less important priority than the day-to-day challenges of simply being an effective teacher in a difficult environment.

Despite their many disappointing experiences with the school system, however, education remains an extremely strong source of hope for families living in persistent poverty. Parents hold on to the hope that their children will have a better life if they succeed in getting a good education.

This article tells the story of one project—called Unleashing Hidden Potential—that aimed to demonstrate that it is possible to bring together teachers and parents living in poverty in a constructive dialog that allows each participant to contribute as well as to learn. During the course of this project, all the participants experience first-hand the challenges as well as the rewards involved in building partnerships aimed at ensuring that all children can learn at school.

Roots of the Project

The roots of the Unleashing Hidden Potential project lie in a thirty-year partnership between the Fourth World Movement and low-income families living in New York City.

In the 1960's, a few European members of a French-based anti-poverty organization were invited to New York to learn about the United States government's War on Poverty. At first these young women worked for War on Poverty programs in the Lower East Side of Manhattan, which was at that time one of the city's poorest areas. After a few years they started their own programs in the Lower East Side. This was the birth of what is now called the Fourth World Movement, the U.S. branch of the International Movement ATD Fourth World. The Fourth World Movement was and continues to be primarily staffed by members of a Fourth World Volunteer Corps, people from many different backgrounds who make a sustained commitment to working with and learning from people who live in persistent poverty.

Through most of the 1970s, Fourth World projects were based in the Lower East Side. They consisted of preschool, after-school programs for children, a drop-in center for young people, summer vacation trips, and "People's University" meetings for parents. At the same time the neighborhood of the Lower East Side was changing. Many of the older tenement buildings were destroyed by fire or condemned and then renovated. The neighborhood became more and more inaccessible to families with low incomes, and many families who had participated in the Fourth World programs were forced to find housing in other parts of the city or even in other cities.

The Fourth World Volunteers kept in contact by visiting families who had moved from the neighborhood. Many of the parents were eager for the Volunteers to continue to work with their children, since they had been part of the preschool or after-school programs in the Lower East Side. At first the Volunteers would read some books or do some craft or learning activity with the children in the families' apartment. Later, however, some of the families suggested that we could do something outdoors, so that other children in the neighborhood could also participate. These were the first New York City Street Libraries. The Street Library program has been a mainstay of the Fourth World's work in New York City ever since.

By the early 1980s Street Libraries were held in four neighborhoods of New York City: the Lower East Side in Manhattan, the South Bronx, and Coney Island and East New York in Brooklyn. In the mid-1980s New York City was undergoing a major crisis of homelessness. As a result, Fourth World Volunteers developed Street Libraries in one "welfare hotel" in Harlem and later in a transitional housing project in Harlem. Through these two Street Libraries many new families got to know and became active participants in the Fourth World Movement.

By the early 1990s the Street Library project was ready for a new step. For years the Street Libraries had been a very mobile project. The project was run out of a van that would travel all around the city, each day of the week to a different location. This allowed the Fourth World Volunteers to get to know different parts of the city and different realities like life in a shelter. The Volunteers came to feel, however, that this formula did not allow enough sustained contact with individual families. In the shelter and the welfare hotel the families came and went frequently. By the time the Volunteers were able to build up a relationship with a family—a process that can take some time—the family might be re-housed in a new area.

In the same way that Fourth World Volunteers twenty years earlier kept in touch with families after they moved from the Lower East Side, the Volunteers also followed families after they moved out of the welfare hotel or the shelter. Several of these families moved into the East New York area of Brooklyn, a neighborhood that already had a well-established Street Library. The Volunteers were able to make connections between families who had moved from the shelter and those who had been living there for some time. East New York was also a significant place to be because of the terrible poverty there. The area had high levels of violence, a serious drug problem, dilapidated housing, and underperforming schools. For all these reasons, the Fourth World Volunteers decided to concentrate the Street Library Program in East New York.

The Street Library in East New York

A Street Library takes place on the sidewalk.[73] Usually the Street Library van arrives in the neighborhood at about the time the neighborhood children get out of school. Some children come right away on their own, but often the Fourth World Volunteers or other Street Library leaders go to the children's homes to invite them and to let their parents know where they will be. At the same time, others are setting up the Street Library, putting out the mobile book case, spreading blankets, starting up the computer, preparing the materials.

A Street Library session usually lasts about two hours. The first hour is centered on books. The children can pick out a book and read on their own or in small groups, and there is usually a time where a story is read out loud for everyone to enjoy.

---

73. Street Libraries can be moved indoors—for example to a community center room or the lobby of an apartment building—in case of cold or inclement weather.

The second half of the Street Library is devoted to group activities. This can be almost anything, setting up a computer database on dinosaurs, painting, making Christmas decorations to take home, or creating flower boxes to use to decorate the street. The most important thing is that the activity be both fun and creative; the idea is that the children should experience the pleasure of learning and working together.

Another key feature of the Street Library is that it must be open to all children, especially those who most need it. The Fourth World Volunteers do not evaluate the success of the Street Library primarily based on *how many* children come, but rather on *which* children come.

It is also crucial that the children's parents be closely linked to the Street Library. Fourth World Volunteers make sure that the parents are aware of what their children are doing in the Street Library, and the Street Library is always open and visible to anyone who wants to see what is happening. Sometimes parents actively participate by reading stories or helping with an activity. Other times they just sit on the stoop nearby and quietly watch. In any case, it is crucial that the parents be able to see what their children are doing, and that the children are aware that their parents support what is happening in the street library.

The Street Library also depends very concretely on the good wishes and advice of the parents. In East New York, for example, the parents suggested where on the block the Street Library should be set up, or where a new Street Library could be developed. Parents also introduce new families and children to the program, and provide practical help by, for example, providing us an outlet to plug in the computer or water to clean up paintbrushes.

Through the Street Libraries, the Fourth World Volunteers got to know a group of families who strongly supported the Street Libraries. These parents also gathered together at events outside of the program—for example in People's Universities, holiday parties, and vacation outings—which helped to create a core of adults who knew each other well and who knew the Fourth World Movement.

The decade of the 1990s was a time of change in East New York. Much like the Lower East Side of Manhattan twenty years earlier, East New York gradually gentrified during the 1990s. Most of the older tenement buildings disappeared and a great deal of new housing was built. The Fourth World Volunteers could see, however, that this process did not help the most disadvantaged families. Even though much of the new housing was designated as "low income housing," it was still out of reach for most of the families who were the mainstays of the Street Library program. Instead of participating in the improvement of their neighborhood, these families often had to leave the neighborhood to find affordable housing in other parts of the city.

The Fourth World Volunteers saw this happening but they were unable to do much about it. They did not have enough contacts in the larger neighborhood to be able to participate fully in discussions about the future of the neighborhood.

A similar situation occurred with the neighborhood schools. The Volunteers could see that the children in the Street Libraries were capable of great things. Yet, at the same time they constantly heard from the children and their parents about how difficult things were for them at school. The children did not seem to learn well at school, and the parents did not have positive relationships with their children's schools and teachers. The Fourth World Volunteers' did make many overtures towards the schools, trying to show what the children were capable of doing. However, building long-term partnerships with the local schools proved to be difficult.

The Fourth World Volunteers' sense of frustration about not being able to affect events that impacted the lives of the children and families we were working with in East New York provided much of the impetus for the Unleashing Hidden Potential project. One Fourth World Volunteer wrote,

> We had Street Libraries in East New York for many years. We had learned a lot with the kids, and we had learned a lot with the parents about how we can work together to make sure that kids love books and that kids learn and develop. What was disappointing to me … was that we had succeeded with a small number of families to achieve something with their kids but it didn't affect the community. It didn't change the way the school worked, it didn't change the way the library worked, it didn't change the image the community at large had of these families.

A New Project in Boston

At a national level, the Fourth World Movement in the United States had a similar desire to be part of the national conversation about persistent poverty and how to overcome it. The Fourth World Volunteers felt the need to share more of what they had learned, to confront their ideas with others doing similar work, and ultimately to have an influence on policies affecting people living in persistent poverty.

In the fall of 1995, two Fourth World Volunteers arrived in Boston to start a new team for Fourth World Movement/USA. Their project was to get to know some important and influential people in the field of poverty. They specifically targeted academics working on poverty-related issues and people and organizations working in the area of community development. For the first year or two this new team concentrated on getting to know the city and trying to identify who could be potential friends and allies. Both of them took classes at some local universities, attended meetings and lectures, and volunteered in local projects. Little by little they got to know more people, and relationships of trust were built.

Over time, however, the team in Boston felt they needed to make another step with their friends. The Volunteers in Boston had learned about what others were doing and saying, and they had introduced many people to the work of the Fourth World Movement. They felt the next step would be to find projects to work on together with some of these new friends.

In 1999, an idea began to take shape. This idea started from a gathering of parents in New York, one of a regular series of meetings the team there had with parents from East New York and a few other parts of the city. For this meeting the team had invited a former Fourth World intern who was then working as a teacher in the New York City public school system.

> We had a very interesting dialog between that teacher, who was teaching in East Harlem, and parents, because she brought a very personal view of what is it to try to be a good teacher and not really succeeding as much as you would like. It was a very different kind of dialog from what regularly happens in schools.

Inspired by that meeting, the U.S. Fourth World Movement decided to create a process in which parents living in poverty could share their ideas about schools and education with "experts" in the field: teachers, academics, and community workers.

For a number of reasons, the Volunteers felt that education was an ideal issue to work on: the Street Library program was educational and well established in East New York;

there was a group of parents who were used to meeting and working together; education was an issue that was of great concern to both the parents and the Fourth World Volunteers; and the country as a whole was also experimenting with ways to improve education for all children.

Preparing the Seminar

From the very beginning the seminar was based on two key principles:

1.   All interested parties in public education—parents, teachers, administrators, academics, community workers, and others—have crucial expertise about education that needs to be part of any dialog that truly aims to improve education for children who have the most difficulties.
2.   In order for such a dialog to be successful, all parties involved in it must want for all voices to be included and must be willing to work over the long term to make sure that in fact all voices are included.

Another key aspect of the seminar was that it would emphasize the voice of parents living in persistent poverty. In the words of one Fourth World Volunteer:

> Usually people do not learn from those in poverty and that is, to our mind, one of the reason why actions against poverty do not work—including education in poor neighborhoods—because they are not informed by those who know poverty best. People never learn from the poor, therefore they do not know how to do it, can be clumsy, even manipulative. On the other hand people among the poorest are not used to teaching, to sharing their wisdom as they never experienced that others gave it value. Therefore much of our efforts had to go into that direction: people in poverty contributing their knowledge to the others.

Workshops in New York

The preparation workshops in New York took place once a month for a period of about one year. Their goal was to prepare the parents to be able to hold their own with professional educators in a discussion on education. The meetings brought out some basic affirmations. For example, at one meeting a mother said, "There's nothing wrong with the minds of our children." This became a rallying cry for the seminar.

The participants at these meetings also did concrete work on education issues. The goal was always to help the parents see that they had a crucial contribution to make, and to work out together what that contribution would be. Here is how one of the organizers of these meeting describes the process:

> At the first workshop, we took a newspaper article from the Daily News that reported about a mother in Brooklyn who was sentenced to three months in jail because she assaulted a teacher. We had a format where one group defends the mom, one group defends the teacher. The two things that were incredible for me that came out were that almost every person in the room had an incident to tell about that they were personally involved in, where there were some serious confrontation between teachers and parents. The second thing was that it was funny because when some of the teachers were playing the role of parents, without realizing it they at some

point were switching back to the role of teacher. We all learned from this that it is hard to put yourself in the shoes or in the role of someone else. And for all the following workshops we tried to dig a bit deeper into the issue. Another time we had a fake radio talk show in which we interviewed the mothers and the teachers and the Fourth World Volunteer. That was a way of showing that we're all experts. We really wanted to push that point: we are all experts. So each time there was a different setting, a different scenario. It was always a little bit fun, never too serious.

Boston

When the Fourth World Volunteers in Boston first started to speak to their academic friends about the idea of a seminar around education using the experience of the Street Library in East New York, many of the academics were eager to join in, to learn more about the project, and to help in thinking about how to present it publicly.

One interesting discussion, for example, centered on this question: How do you demonstrate, or "prove," that the Street Library is successful? The Fourth World Volunteers and the parents of the children who participate were all convinced that it is successful in many ways, but the academics pushed us to go further in trying to explain exactly where the successes were, and to look more closely at what was happening to make it successful. Some academic showed that one way to "prove" the success of the Street Library project would be to look at it from different perspectives or points of view. This idea became another key foundation of the Unleashing Hidden Potential project. We would look at the Street Library experience from different points of view: parents, teachers, children, Fourth World volunteers and academics. Each person was an expert in his or her own way. Everyone could begin to understand the impact of the Street Libraries through looking at them from many different points of view.

The Roads Come Together

Little by little the parents in New York and the academics in Boston started to get to know each other. It was good for each group to have time to prepare first on their own, but for the eventual success of the seminar they had to get to know each other at least a little bit, before the actual event. Part of this was just getting to know each other as individuals, but partly it was to practice the kind of dialog and mutual learning that would take place at the seminar. Some academics came down to New York to attend the parent workshops, one or two at a time. And some parents traveled to Boston to visit some of the projects of the academics.

This is an account of one of those visits:

One visit [in Boston] was at the Eliot Pearson Experimental Elementary School at Tufts University. One academic who had been part of the process all along invited the group to observe a class and then discuss what they had seen. Parents were fascinated by the quality of the school, wanting to register their children immediately! The teacher who had been observed with the class came to the meeting after her class. She was stunned by the astuteness of the parents' observations. One mother for example marveled at the fact that these five year olds poured water for one another themselves for their painting projects. It is so important for a child to learn by doing, to have the responsibility for serving water and taking the risk to spill it all over the paintings. They commented that they could never do that in their homes nor in their schools, where life is too chaotic. This prevents children from experimenting and learning. The teacher had never expected inner-city women, with their reputation of being uninterested in their children's education, to appreciate her work so much and she right away asked to participate in the seminar. A year after the seminar she had some participants come to the class she teaches to student teachers.

Preparatory Papers

Early on the preparation committee decided that one of the "conditions" for participating in the seminar would be that each person would have to write a paper. The theme of this paper was, "Describe something you have done to try to help in the education of a child who was having trouble learning."

Most of the parents wrote about their own children, and the teachers were easily able to find examples among their own students. The academics, however, tended at first to write about examples from their research or about other educators they knew about. The Volunteers, however, pushed everyone to write about their own personal experiences. The idea was that these papers would put all the participants on a similar footing. Each person's efforts would be evident, but in the face of trying to work with an individual child in difficulty no one would be able to claim to have easy answers. It was also hoped that these papers would bring out different kinds of expertise. The parents would show how they struggle to help their own children, while teachers, community workers or academics would contribute different experiences and training.

For everyone the challenge was to look deeply at these experiences of trying to help children in need in order to gain from them lessons that could help others. We asked people to start by looking at successes. What worked? Why? The goal was also for all the writers to try to look beyond the actual experiences, and the apparent successes, to see what could have been done differently. We wanted everyone to be proud of their successes, but also self-confident enough to be able to look critically at themselves.

The Unleashing Hidden Potential Seminar

The seminar took place in November 2000 in a relaxed rural setting a couple of hours outside of New York City. There were a total of about 50 people for the four days. The time was organized around different kinds of opportunities to meet and interact with the others, in meetings but also in practical workshops, at meals, and in informal times. Everyone would get the opportunity to contribute in different ways and with different people through two different kinds of small groups: "peer groups" and "mixed groups."

Some basic ground rules were set out for the seminar. All participants should have written a preparatory paper and have read those of the others. There would be no titles used at the seminar; everyone would use first names. The proceedings were organized around the basic belief that all children can learn. Everyone should be open to getting to know and to listen to the other participants, and should accept that the goal of the seminar was to engage in a mutual exploration and that it would take time to work through these complex issues—in other words, no easy answers!

The main structure of the seminar was "learning from stories." Four stories were presented: one by a teacher, one by a parent, one by two members of the New York team who had worked on Street Libraries, and one from a young man who had participated in Street Libraries when he was a child. Each of these stories was presented by the writer to the whole group. Then two people gave a pre-prepared reaction to the story, followed by further discussion in the mixed groups.

Following are excerpts from the four main stories that were presented during the seminar.

A Parents' Perspective

I am a mother of four children and we live in a city housing project. I met the Fourth World Movement eight or nine years ago. I got involved because my kids were drawn to the Street Library, and I wasn't paying much attention to my kids at the time. I did little things with the kids, but I would be out in my own world until I started watching my kids in the Street Library. I started to think, "What do they find so interesting?" I looked at the other Fourth World Volunteers and I didn't want anybody to say anything bad to them because it was too good to be true that they were around and were giving the kids something to do. I started to get involved little by little until I felt good about being involved. It became a family tradition; it became family with my family. It was probably one of the most positive, motivating forces that came into my life at that particular time.

There are so many distractions in the street that it seems like it would be hard for the Street Library to get the kids' attention. It is hard sometimes, but not only do they get the kids' attention, they keep their attention. I believe that comes from the Fourth World Volunteers building a personal relationship with the kids, expressing concern for them, and letting them experience some undivided attention. The volunteers ignore the environment around them and they do their Street Library. Never mind if a bomb goes off when they are reading with the kids! Sometimes there are a lot of negative activities happening, and the Street Library continues to capture and maintain the interest of the kids they are working with. Sometimes, kids will get pulled away by things that happen around them. They'll look up and then they'll be right back into what they were doing with the Street Library. I think that is because the volunteers don't let their attention go away. I think a lot of kids feel it's much better to be with the Street Library where it's nice and peaceful, and where they're feeling wanted, than to be some place where there is cursing and yelling. The Street Library creates a very good, positive atmosphere for the kids and parents who become involved. Everything done with the kids in a positive environment, in a positive way, helps.

I think that teachers and the educational system can try to help these kids better by building a relationship with the kids so that they know where the kids are coming from on the inside. School is not a bad thing, it's just that the kids have to feel that they're wanted in school and not just that, "We have to go." They have to feel like, "You want me to be here in school," and for the right reasons, for positive reasons. They have to want to go to school like they want to go to the Street Library.

Teachers could take a little bit more time to build a relationship with their students and not just say, "You haven't learned this, you don't know that, you didn't do your homework." In the morning, when the students first come in, instead of saying, "Alright, take out your books," teachers could take a few minutes to break the ice by saying, "Good morning. How do you feel today? Did you sleep well?" You don't have to go deep, just let the kids know that you care about them and then discuss the homework. You have to treat the kids like you want them to learn. You have to want them to grow and be nurtured positively.

My seven-year-old daughter, Nakyshia, cries when she is changing her teachers. She falls in love with the teacher. She finds good things, she even finds bad things, but she builds a relationship. She is at the top of her grade. I think it is because she builds a relationship. She isn't just trying to learn. She tries to understand. She didn't get to the top of her class just by memorizing. That's what impresses me most about my daughter. She builds a relationship with her educational environment and with everything she does. She wants to understand everything. She breaks things down: "Well, why does this get to be connected to that in order for this to work?"

A Teacher's Perspective

The hardest reality I faced each year as a junior high school social studies teacher in East Harlem was realizing that there would be students who couldn't be "reached" and who would fall through the cracks. For these students the teacher-parent or parent-child relationship did not work well. Not reaching all the kids aggravated and depressed my spirit immensely.

My best success in gaining respect and helping children learn was when I involved them in projects, activities, or lessons where I shared my personal convictions, values, or passions. I created a recycling program in the school. Students and staff would recycle paper, bottles, and cans during the week and then once a week, students would go and empty the special bins and take them to a drop-off point for the custodians to place outside on recycling day. Students really loved the idea that they were helping the environment and also loved seeing an adult who truly cared about the issue. This simple project taught the kids that they could make a difference. We were truly rewarded when we won the Sanitation Department's "Team Up to Clean Up" contest this year at the district, borough, and city-wide level.

Another part of my success came from living in the community and being involved with residents in many other community activities. I came to understand families' circumstances much better. Also, by paying attention to any information of my students' backgrounds, I was able to place their problems in a broader context of their personal and societal struggles. Living in East Harlem didn't mean I automatically gained all students' respect in school, but many of my students appreciated knowing that I was genuinely concerned. It often surprised my students to see me shopping in the grocery store or jogging past them in the hours after school. I became more real to my students and worth a bit more of their time when they would see me in school the next day.

Two Fourth World Volunteers' Perspective

Fourth World Volunteers have succeeded, together with many parents, at creating and running Street Libraries in different places in New York. We arrived ten years ago and took over from other volunteers. We were welcomed by the children, their parents and their community. We discovered how much these children want to learn and how passionate they can all be. We discovered how dedicated their parents and their community are. But we didn't discover this overnight. It took us a long time to understand.

In 1992, we were invited by Ms. Price to start a new Street Library in East New York. She had seen us using a computer with children in the street, and she wanted us to come to her block.

We didn't know anybody in this new place. We only knew from Ms. Price and Mr. Elijah that the children of the community were surrounded by drug activities and the consequences of it. We also knew that Ms. Price and Mr. Elijah saw the computer as a way to give the children something else. "We can do something against drugs and we should get together to stop it. Bringing the computer into the street helps" Ms. Price introduced us to a dozen families from her community and we started to come every week with our blanket, books and a computer. Ms. Price would sit next to us, watching what we were doing and making sure all the children would get a turn on the computer.

It was obvious from the beginning that we would not have been able to be there without the trust and the protection of Ms. Price. It's hard to say whether we had any other choice, but we clearly made the choice to rely on Ms. Price and Mr. Elijah. We relied on their trust, their authority, their advice. Later on, we were able to rely on other parents as well.

There are many things that affect the way children are able to read books with us or participate in the activity we bring to them. [...]But nothing can disturb a Street Library more than when children feel that their parents are disrespected. Some comments quickly lead to arguments. "Your mother had to borrow some milk yesterday. Your mother came to beg for a cigarette. Your mother is a crack-head." That's enough to create a fight and bring the Street Library to a stop.

Children can't learn if their parents are looked down on. When that happens, they think that everything is wrong with them, because your parents are always a part of yourself. The way your parents are looked at is also how you are looked at. The children saw that we could recognize the value of their parents.

Trying to listen to the parents and the children was a key to creating a learning atmosphere, and a fruitful relationship. We always wanted parents to participate more in the Street Library. Sometimes parents were sitting on the stairs 20 feet away from us and we were thinking, "Why don't they come sit with us and read with the kids?" But one of them told us another day, "I really like what you are doing with the kids. If I can sit outside to support you, I will." It made us understand that parents supported us in ways that we didn't see. Sitting on the stairs 20 feet away was an act of support. It was not the support we expected, but it had an important influence on the way children behaved during the Street Library. Children didn't come to the Street Library by accident. Their parents prepared and sent them. This was their first involvement.

In the Street Library we try to create this basic rule: No children are kicked out of the Street Library or put off to the side. It is not easy for children to accept everyone but they know that's the way the Street Library is. Even if we have to send a child home one day, we are never going to say, "This kid can't be a part of the Street Library." If a child says, "Oh, he doesn't like to read," or, "He's smelly," we don't go into that, we sit next to the child, read with him and enjoy the time together. If children say, "He can't type on the computer," then we start the computer activity with the child they are insulting.

We will go first to pick up the children who are more excluded. This sends a message that we are there for everyone. I think that parents know who we are coming for. It doesn't mean that the Street Library is only for the children who can't read yet, but we give them a certain priority.

We often start a Street Library with informal reading. We sit on the blanket, take a book and try to create interest around it. A few children sit next to us to listen to the story. Often, after a couple of pages, one child would say, "Oh, I want to read, I want to read!" I would say, "No, I'm reading the book," because if I let this child read aloud, children who can't read at their age level are going to leave. They will be embarrassed. I often impose myself and don't let the other child read. Maybe it doesn't sound very educational but it allows me to keep all the children around the book. Later on, there is always a time when the child who can read already will read, but first we have to create an atmosphere for all the children to be comfortable.

Perspective of a Street Library Participant

When I graduated from high school three years ago, I thought of all my family and what they had done for me to get there. I am the first one in my extended family to have graduated from high school.

I also remember [in the Street Library] there was a big wooden book, with wheels that opened like a book and inside there were children's books. I think about that book sometimes! My aunts were taking me to this program. There were no other such programs around. I guess my grandfather thought that it was the right thing for us to do. And Vincent[74] was a friend of the family. That was important too.

There were no books in our home. Maybe a little book here and there, but not really books for us kids to read. My daughter, now she's two, and she already has plenty of books. She is not growing up in anything like what I grew up in. I want to make sure that she is not exposed to extreme poverty, or overwhelmed by a lot of people, or roaches and rats, you know.

---

74. Vincent is one of the Fourth World Volunteers who was in the New York team at that time.

In the Street Library, they taught us a lot of things. Everyone who went there, we were all rough edged. I mean that we had rough abilities. The potential was there, but you just had to teach us, because we were not learning in the streets. In the Street Library, they understood that.

For kids to succeed, you have to stress how important the family is. Everything they do is going to reflect on the family. So if they learn how to read and write, that is going to reflect on the family as a whole, in a positive way. If they commit a crime, it's going to reflect in a bad way. Kids will make big efforts if you tell them that, because they want their families to be proud.

I am proud of my family. I know one thing: it has been a struggle. But the family stays together. I am proud of that the most, that within the family everybody cares for each other. If nobody cares about you it is not worthwhile to struggle. You do something because there is something at the end of the tunnel, because others count on you.

Teachers have to reinforce that family pride. That is what Fourth World Movement did for me. The Fourth World Volunteers, they always showed a lot of respect for my family, for my grandfather.

They helped me get a sense of history, of the big picture. They helped me see who my grandfather really was. He was a symbol. To me, he was like Moses. He led us into the unknown, to give us a better chance. He came from Puerto Rico, not knowing what to expect, to let us have a chance at making it. He probably saw the big picture. Coming from Puerto Rico to the US was taking a chance. Moses never saw the Promised Land and my grandpa never saw his family getting out of poverty. Martin Luther King never saw interracial couples walking down the street like we do now as an everyday thing. But he started the dream; he started taking the steps forward so this could take place. My grandfather never saw me graduating from high school. He was the one starting me in that direction to show me how important it was, and how important the family is, so that's why I have those values today. And I am going to pass it on to my daughter. I think that it's also the teachers' and educators' job to express that sense to the kids, to give an overall view of how people slowly move ahead.… Not everybody is going to see the dream, but somebody starts the steps, starts the train moving, then generations get better and better and then you see the dream.

Seminar Workshops

There were workshops each day of the seminar: singing, a puzzle-learning game, creating things with paper, and helping to make a CD-ROM. These were a chance for participants to relax and to get to know each other in different ways.

One workshop was group singing. One of the seminar organizers wrote,

> The leader of the singing workshop is a math teacher and is in charge of training of all math teachers in his city. The injustice of low math achievement for minority youth is both his life struggle and his constant source of discouragement. He was not sure he wanted to devote four days of vacation to despair even more. His other passion is helping people sing together as a choir—no matter how well they think they can sing—convinced him to come and run such a workshop. Not only did he succeed in having the whole group sign a difficult and beautiful song, but the very experience became for him and the whole group a common experience of helping each other learn, and a metaphor of what happens in his math class.

Small Groups

The small groups were also a key element in the seminar. One set of small groups—the "mixed groups"—met after each of the four main presentations, to discuss and share ideas about what had been presented. There were also two times during the four days when people met in "peer groups," parents, teachers, academics or community workers. These various groups allowed significant issues to come to the surface.

For example, one discussion concerned how to share the seminar experience with others who were not there. During the course of the four days people started to realize that they were experiencing something unique, and that it would be important to share this beyond the 50 participants. One participant suggested that what was needed was to make a kind of "recipe book." He felt that the Street Libraries and the seminar itself were extremely significant and that the group should work together on writing down how others could replicate similar experiences. Some other participants felt that approach was a bit too simplistic.

One parent, for example, wrote afterwards about this question,

> And from this four-day seminar it was said that maybe from our experience we could make a tool for others to use, to help them. But it is not a cook book. You cannot use this as a recipe. You can not just take our situation and make it work in your situation. It will not work; people, places, they are different. It is a tool to start conversations and to let you know that these are some of the things that can happen.

This question has been an ongoing theme since the time of the seminar. All the participants felt that important lessons were learned throughout the seminar and the preparation process, and that these lessons should be shared widely. At the same time, however, the participants were also aware of how much time, care and effort went into the preparation of this event, and they knew that not all other groups would be able to replicate that. The key is to take from the experience some basic principles and to see how these might be transferred to other circumstances and other settings.

After the Seminar

In the years following the Unleashing Hidden Potential seminar, the participants continued the dynamic of the seminar in a variety of ways. The parents in New York continued to support their local Street Libraries and to meet together around the theme of education. Some of the academics wrote about the seminar or introduced the Fourth World volunteers to others who were working on similar themes or projects. The Fourth World Movement produced a series of newsletters about the project and spoke at several public gatherings about the seminar and the process that led to it.

One of the most significant outcomes of the seminar is an interactive CD-ROM that gathers most of the stories that were shared before, during and after the seminar. The CD-ROM is intended to be used as a conversation starter, so that others can also institute dialogs about how to improve education for children who need it most.

This CD-ROM has been used in a variety of settings. It was shown, for example, to an influential educational policy organization in Washington, D.C., to a group of teachers in Appalachia, and to a class of teachers-in-training in New York City.

The CD-ROM was also used during a series of one-day training sessions for a group of beginning teachers in New Jersey. These teachers were all recruited to teaching through what is called "alternate routes," which means that they did not go through traditional teacher training in college. These teachers are obliged, during their first year in the classroom, to attend evening and weekend classes that are designed to support them in their new profession. Many of these teachers are also assigned to hard-to-staff schools in some of the poorest areas of the state. A person who was running the evening and weekend classes for these alternate route teachers heard about the Unleashing Hidden Potential CD-ROM and asked the Fourth World Volunteers to run workshops for these new teachers about parent-teacher relationships using the Unleashing Hidden Potential CD-ROM.

At one of these workshops, each of the new teachers was asked to give one word to describe the parents of their students. Some of the words they chose were "overwhelmed," "underprivileged," "uninterested," "aggressive," "defensive," "frustrated," "clueless," and "marginalized." Some of the teachers also chose more positive words: "supportive," "determined," and "encouraging."

Soon afterwards, one of the parents who had participated in the Unleashing Hidden Potential seminar spoke about some of her own experiences with teachers, and about some of the parent meetings she attended where parents shared their experiences about teachers. She revealed that parents often use some of the very same words—both positive and negative—when speaking about teachers that the teachers used when speaking about parents.

Workshops such as this one are not able to re-create in a few hours what the original seminar created over a much longer period of time. However, the CD-ROM is a tool that can help to start conversations and stimulate ideas that can continue to grow over time.

Conclusion

The United States has a well-justified reputation for having some of the finest schools in the world. The same educational system that produces these fine schools, however, also has far too many schools that are struggling to meet even the most basic standards. There are of course many reasons for this, and just as many possible and proposed solutions. This paper aims to shed light on one aspect of the fight for equal educational opportunity for all: the desire of parents living in persistent poverty to be full partners in their children's educations.

As we have seen, researchers and lawmakers have recognized that parent participation is a key factor in school improvement. Assuring the participation of low-income parents, however, is far from being realized.

In the most underprivileged schools, parents and teachers alike are under a great deal of pressure. Unfortunately, what too often results is that everyone tries to find someone else to blame. Parents hope desperately that their children will not repeat their own school failures, and when they see their children struggling in school they often lash out at the teachers. Teachers are often ill-prepared to deal with conditions they find in high poverty schools, and teachers in these schools are often less trained and less experienced than teachers in other schools.[75] In these circumstances, teachers can accuse the parents of their students of being bad parents, of not even caring about their children's education. In the face of these conflicting accusations the ones who suffer most are the children.

---

75. For more about the inequitable distribution of teachers in U.S. schools, see "Honor in the Boxcar," by the Education Trust, available at: http://www2.edtrust.org/NR/rdonlyres/E0A47827-6FA9-4BAD-A157-60ABB852F51A/0/k16_spring2000.pdf.

The Unleashing Hidden Potential seminar does not promise any simple solutions to the problems facing our nations' schools. It does show, however, that it is possible for people from very different backgrounds and very different perspectives to put aside their differences and seriously try to work together for the benefit of children.

The barriers to be overcome can be formidable. One of the seminar participants, an academic, wrote, "I was scared of being with 'welfare mothers.' I was scared I would have nothing to tell them and that we would not have anything to speak to each other about." In fact, this woman did meet "welfare mothers" during the seminar, and she had a long conversation with one mother that both of them often fondly referred to afterwards. This was what the seminar was all about, fostering encounters between people who might otherwise never meet around a common desire to improve education for all children.

In the words of one teacher:

> It was the parents coming to view the teachers as human beings with lives and problems just as teachers are learning that parents have lives and problems and certainly that children do. The more there is a sense of everyone working together and communicating and talking, the more a child's learning can be positively impacted.

CHAPTER 8

Another Approach to Poverty Indicators in Belgium

Johan Bellens, Régis De Muylder, Béatrice Meurant,
Henk Van Hootegem, and Frank Vereecken[76]

This chapter reproduces the synthesis of a report with the same title published by the Service de Lutte Contre la Pauvreté, la Précarité et l'Exclusion Sociale du Centre pour l'Egalité des Chances et la Lutte Contre le Racisme (Centre for Equality of Opportunity and the War on Racism) in Brussels. The objective of the report was to conduct indepth work with families living in extreme poverty on how indicators for assessing poverty could be improved in Belgium. The report resulted from a two-year program that gathered 23 participants, including 12 who live in poverty chosen from Belgian NGOs that give the poor a chance to express their opinions. The other participants were academics, representatives of various government bodies and institutions, and the pedagogical team. The chapter provides insights on how poverty indicators could be improved to better reflect the reality of the life of the poor.

The question of updating the qualitative and quantitative indicators of poverty is addressed in the "Cooperative Accord for Policy Continuity in the War on Poverty"[77] in the following terms:

---

76. The whole report in French is available on www.luttepauvrete.be. Summaries are available in English, German and Dutch.

77. *Cooperative accord between the Federal State, the Communities and the Regions concerning continuity in poverty policy*, signed in Brussels, 5th May 1998, approved by the Flemish Community, "Belgian Monitor" 16 December 1998, by the Federal State, the German-speaking Community, the Walloon Region, the Brussels Capital Region, "Belgian Monitor" 10 January 1999.

after consultation with the scientific community, government bodies and the competent institutions, the social partners and those organizations within which the most impoverished persons express themselves, the signatory parties will examine those quantitative and qualitative indicators which may be used and/or further developed in order to analyze evolution in every field (connected with poverty and with the war on poverty), in such a way as to enable the appropriate authorities to intervene in the most suitable way.

(Art. 3)

This cooperative accord, and thus also the Article relative to indicators, is one of the results arising from the *General Report on Poverty*[78] (GRP), which, for Belgium, was innovative on two essential levels. On the one hand, the classic conception of poverty—low level of revenues and consumption—was considerably enlarged in the report, being expressed more in terms of human rights violations. On the other hand, the report was drawn up cooperatively by all the parties concerned; in particular, populations well below the poverty line were implicated through the medium of the associations which represent them.

Effective efforts have been made to determine those indicators that most adequately take into account the reality of poverty in all its complexity, such as within the framework of national plans for social inclusion. However, associations representing the poor are concerned about the low level of involvement of actual poor populations in such efforts. To improve this, they have drawn up a research-action-training program, which public authorities have agreed to support.

Their argumentation rests on the insufficiency of the classic poverty indicators used. Here is a summary of the main aspects:

- Current indicators do not take daily reality, as it is experienced by the poor, sufficiently into account, whether quantitatively or qualitatively.
- The poorest people are barely being reached by the statistical mechanisms deployed.
- The parameters used are generally not well adapted to the least favored populations.
- Those "technical difficulties" advanced as a reason for the absence of the very poor from these statistics actually indicate a general lack of interest and consideration for their position.
- The data given is open to manipulation for economic or political reasons.
- In addition, some of the indicators currently used have the effect of stigmatizing certain categories of people, causing these to be afraid of expressing themselves and to develop an attitude of mistrust toward the rest of society.[79]

The issue of the participation of the populations concerned in the drawing up of poverty indicators is a crucial one. Although poverty studies and projects sometimes consult poor populations for information, these are practically never associated with the interpretation or use of such data.

---

78. *Rapport Général sur la Pauvreté* (General report on Poverty) (1994), ATD Quart Monde, Belgian Union of Towns and Communes (CPAS section), King Baudouin Foundation, Brussels.

79. The complete argumentation of these associations is published in extenso in: Service de Lutte contre la pauvreté, la précarité et l'exclusion sociale (2001), *En dialogue, six ans après le Rapport Général sur la Pauvreté, Premier rapport bisannuel*, Centre pour l'égalité des chances et la lutte contre le racisme (Centre for Equality of Opportunity and the War on Racism) Bruxelles. http://www.luttepauvrete.be/rapportbisannuel.htm

Goals of the Research-Action-Training and Method

1. Find those parameters which best take into account reality as experienced by the poor when drawing up the indicators.
2. Enable the very poor to participate in all of this research, in collaboration with others concerned by the problem of poverty.

The two goals are intimately linked: to comprehend daily reality in poor communities, it was necessary to have the experience of poor people, as expressed by themselves, as a reference point, as well as to engage their participation in all the stages of the program, from its design to the drawing up of the final report.

The second goal refers us also to Article 3 of the cooperative accord, where it is a question of mobilizing the parties concerned.

The method retained to enable the dialog and participation of the different actors was the merging of different types of knowledge. This program involved those actually living in poverty working together with the scientists and the representatives of the various government bodies and institutions to create the conditions necessary to ensure that the knowledge and experience of each could interact and contribute to a common reflection on the concept and use of poverty indicators.

There were 23 program participants, 12 of whom live in poverty. These latter were chosen from among those associations within which the poor can express their opinions. The participants came from the country's three regions. A pedagogical team, responsible for the project, was charged with the mission of regulating the tasks. This team consisted of a coordinator, and evaluator, an administrative collaborator and two pedagogical associates. The role of these last two persons consisted in supporting those project participants living in poverty and guaranteeing the presence of those conditions necessary for their full participation.

Results

The Dialog and the Choice of Subjects Requiring Closer Examination

A dialog took place between the participants, permitting a constructive exchange that served as a basis for joint proposals. This is a result in and of itself. Several of the participants remarked at the end of the program that this dialog presented a kind of reciprocal training in which each was able to learn from the others. This is without ignoring the difficulties typical of such dialogs; in particular those linked with the participation of persons from poor backgrounds.

The choice of themes that were examined may be considered as a result. Indeed, since the time available for this project was limited, it was impossible, within the context of the method retained, to cover all the subjects connected with poverty. Therefore, even some important themes could not be broached.

Among the subjects chosen—financial aspects; work and employment; the application of rights; human sentiments—some might seem surprising in a project devoted to poverty indicators. The choice arises from the participants' desire to consistently use the experience of poor people as a reference. Despite the obvious difficulties associated with certain themes, they were retained because of their importance to the life of poor people.

Financial Aspects

It is usual to define poverty in reference to an income level: those households that do not attain this level are considered poor. A "threshold" is fixed. The threshold most commonly used in the Belgian and European context is 60 percent of average income.[80] Such a threshold is arbitrary and fails badly to take the real experience of poverty into account. It does not help us to understand either the real significance, or grasp the implications, of living from one day to the next on a very low income.

Living with a limited income does not permit people to meet all their essential needs and, consequently, imposes choices among these and the renunciation of some of them. This is an essential reality for poor people. Another important characteristic of poor populations is the level of debt. From our reflection emerged the importance of distinguishing between two types of debt. The first concerns debts linked to consumer goods, which are indeed not characteristic to any particular segment of society. The second concerns the payment of certain specific charges: gas or electricity bill, school expenses, health costs—particularly hospitalization. This second type of debt is far more characteristic of poor segments of society and possesses the particularity, not found in the case of consumer product debt, of touching their fundamental rights. Analysis disclosed two further realities concerning financial aspects. First, the proportion of the available budget devoted to accommodation is often considerable among the poor, something confirmed by the national enquiry into household budgets. Second, school expenses are also a significant budgetary item, even though there are disparities under this heading, depending on the type of education.

In order to complete and add nuance to the existing indicators, the participants recommend:

- Calculate the proportion of the household budget destined to cover accommodation (including the cost of water, gas and electricity services), that proportion needed to cover all debts and that which is required to cover school expenses (including transport to and from school);
- Identify, among the total debt, those debts which are linked to fundamental rights;
- Calculate the "available budget." If one subtracts from the total income that part which pays for accommodation and that which must be set aside for debt repayment—two significant sums, the non-payment of which represents a real danger to poor people, one arrives at the "available budget" for the meeting of all other needs (food, clothing, healthcare, transport, leisure, education, and so forth). This available budget can be calculated. To attempt to give a better account of its value for a given household, it is suggested to compare this sum with the average amount spent by households of the same size. Evaluating the "available budget" in this way contributes to a realization of the difficulties experienced by poor households to ensure their essential needs.

---

80. To calculate median income, all revenues are classified, from the least to the largest and the average is taken. Because this is in relation to family size, alterations are made according to the size of the household.

Employment and Work

Employment may be one means by which to improve one's standard of living, but this is not automatically so. Certainly this is not true for the underemployed or those whose working statute is precarious. For people living in poverty, a job should enable them to plan for the future and to improve their standard of living in a lasting way. To enable this, a "steady" job is required, a term for which the participants gave the following criteria:

- it should include a working contract which clearly regulates the duties and obligations of each party;
- it should be adequately paid;
- it should give access to social security and all of those rights envisaged under current employment legislation;
- it should have a guarantee of duration;
- it should take into account the obstacles inherent to the lives of poor people; and
- it should be chosen by the worker him/herself.

Among the obstacles to employment encountered in poor neighborhoods, the participants listed:

- the difficulty of having their particular competences and work experience accepted at their just value, given that the poor usually have little in the way of education/ qualification, but rather a variety of experience gained in precarious employment;
- elements linked to the difficulties of life in poverty, such as health problems, the question of child day-care, transport;
- specific additional costs may be linked with having a job: transport, clothing, and so forth; and
- the fact of having worked outside the habitual routine of normal employment, or having been in prolonged inactivity.

In the face of such obstacles support and assistance are necessary; it should be possible to say to what measure these are available within the framework of a given job.

These findings gave rise to the following proposals on the issue of employment:

- The "administrative" benchmarks currently used to measure the level of unemployment are rendering a whole class of people, who are indeed without work, invisible; we must take the situation of these people into account. One path suggested in the program is the evaluation of the "reserve of manpower."[81]
- A "level of stable employment" should be calculated, with reference to how many criteria (from among the six suggested) are effectively fulfilled by any given job.
- Where social assistance measures are suggested, they should be evaluated with regard to how well they contribute to the autonomy of the worker concerned.

---

81. See notably: Laffut M., Ruyters C. (2002), *Tentative d'évaluation du sous-emploi et de la réserve de main d'oeuvre latente en Belgique et dans les trois régions*, in: Capital humain et dualisme sur le marché du travail, Coll. Economie-Société-Marché, De Boeck Université, pp. 169–195.

With regard to vocational training, poor people are sometimes under the impression that such measures are, for the most part, intended to "occupy" the unemployed, to exercise a form of control over them, yet are of little real help with finding or regaining employment. Training courses should be systematically evaluated with the aid of indicators, to determine who has access to them, who truly participates and, above all, what has become—in the short-, medium-, and long-term—of the person who has taken such a course.

The question of employment support was also analyzed by the participants. In certain cases this looks more like an aid to the company concerned in the form of a subsidy granted (nominally as a reward for having provided a job), rather than a trampoline into the world of regular work for an unemployed person. Studies have shown the limited, even perverse, effects of some measures of this type: such as aid being earmarked for a certain category of unemployed person, to the detriment of others who, while they may not qualify for this particular measure, are sometimes in an even more vulnerable situation. The intention here is not to denigrate all forms of employment subsidy, but to encourage a rigorous assessment of their effects, through constant systematic evaluation, rather than through occasional studies.

To better illuminate the link between employment and poverty, the notion of a person's employment history is important. The participants recommend that means be provided to take this history into account. The Banque Carrefour contains employment and social security data. In the current state of affairs, consulting this data does not reveal employment history, the data being both incomplete and hard to access. Certain improvements should be introduced, within the respect of confidentiality and ethics, to enable the inclusion and availability of employment history.

The Application of Rights

In the followup to the GRP—and therefore also to the cooperative accord—which recognized that vulnerability and the impossibility of exercising rights or of assuming responsibilities constitute essential dimensions of poverty, the participants wished to get to the core of the question of rights. They noted that there are already current indicators that are linked with certain rights, such as those concerning health, education or housing. These indicators enable us to describe a certain number of realities at the heart of a population.

Nevertheless, people living in poverty frequently encounter difficulties in attaining their rights. This is why, instead of opting for a vertical approach to rights (that is to say, one after another, area by area), the participants have taken a horizontal one (that is to say, common to the entirety of rights in question) and chosen specifically to deepen the question of the operation of such rights.

The poor frequently find themselves in a weak position with regard to their rights; very often they must fulfill certain conditions to be sure of having their fundamental rights respected. Thus normally guaranteed rights become, for poor people, conditional rights. The obstacle race which leads to the obtaining of a right is often complex—and is not always successful in achieving its goal. The efforts made by poor people to obtain their rights become manifest: they themselves often refer to it as an "ongoing struggle." Taking a series of real-life situations as points of departure, the participants have identified five stages in this obstacle race:

■ Information: this is less a question of knowing what ones rights are as of understanding the social mechanisms to attain them;

■ Taking initial steps: elements such as previous negative experience, suspicion, fear of possible repercussions, feeling oneself to be of no consequence, all these constitute obstacles which may lead a poor person to give up on their initial intention;

■ Proceeding with the intention: involves aspects such as the kind of reception, expressing and officially registering the request, the cost and time involved;

■ The result of these efforts: has the sought after right been attained? In what time frame? Was the response adequate? What are the consequences of the suggested response? Indeed, in certain cases, the response given may involve negative consequences for the life of the person concerned or that of their family;

■ Eventual measures of recourse in the face of a decision taken.

Designing instruments that take into account and evaluate all these stages is difficult. The participants have uncovered certain paths to be followed which are discussed in the text, but these still require further reflection.

It is not unusual for poor people to be erased from administrative archives. We need to evaluate the scale of this phenomenon, inasmuch as it represents a state of absolute denial of rights. However, administrative erasure is not necessarily linked to poverty and we should take this into account if we are to avoid confounding two situations which are, in their nature, distinct from one another.

Solidarity is a force that exists in poorer quarters, just as it may exist in other neighborhoods. The participants have laid bare certain situations in which the virtue of solidarity comes into conflict with the realization of rights. This seems to them to be an anomaly that first needs to be identified if it is to be corrected.

Human Sentiments

Why have we broached this issue in a work devoted to poverty indicators? There are two principle reasons. Emotions play an important role in the life of the poor. Also, it is important to take sentiments into account if we are to understand poor people, their life experience and how they deal with it.

To describe these sentiments, various approaches were taken. This led the participants to ask themselves the question: are there certain emotions that are characteristic of poverty. The reply was negative: every emotion may be felt by any human being. That which is characteristic of poor segments of society is the intensity and, above all, the accumulation of such feelings. The participants demonstrated the importance of considering the chain of cause and effect: the situation which a person experiences as the source of the emotion, the way the emotion manifests itself and what the reaction is.

How to speak about feelings? For the participants, the importance is not to find a measure: attempts to quantify a feeling of well-being or the use of scales—such as the suicide rate, or the rate of psychotropic drug use—seem inadequate to them when seeking to express human feelings with regard to poverty. These emotions should be taken into account because of their importance in the life of poor people. The question was asked whether surveys might be used to contribute to this consideration of sentiments. This reflection was enlarged, inasmuch as surveys are frequently used tools in the study of realities experienced within a population, particularly realities connected with poverty. The representatives of government bodies and the scientists tended to be in favor of this approach, an investigative tool with which they are familiar. The poor, however, seemed rather more suspicious of surveys. There is little definitive agreement on this issue, though most of the group supported a number of reflections concerning such surveys:

- Questions are not always pertinent to the experience of the poor.
- Questions may be ambiguous, badly drawn up or hard to understand.
- The gathering method (whether the respondent is asked to reply in writing or is directly interviewed by a field worker) may be an obstacle.
- Within statistical samples representing the entirety of the population, the very poor are under-represented, rendering less reliable any results concerning them.
- Temporary events having nothing to do with the enquiry may influence the reply, which is not taken into account during interpretation.
- The interpretation of replies is a delicate matter to be undertaken with caution.
- Analyses and interpretations are undertaken by persons exterior to the situation, leaving the poor person concerned no possibility to intervene at this stage.

General Reflections

Certain elements bring together all the discrete topics, the different aspects of life being interconnected. Towards the end of their work, the participants broached three important points that emerge from the totality of subjects tackled during the program.

- *Watchdog groups:* To construct poverty indicators, we refer to administrative and other data and gather information in different ways. After this, the data gathered is subjected to analysis and interpretation before being put to use. The entire process calls for considerable vigilance, both in the way that we speak of poverty and the way we evaluate the policies of the war on poverty, if the results are to concord with the real life experience of poor people. How can we ensure such vigilance, if not through the creation of watchdog committees in which people who actually live below the poverty line are effectively represented?
- *Accumulation and chain reaction:* Serious poverty always concerns several areas of existence. That which affects one area has repercussions on the others (chain reaction effect). This reality put a finger on one of the inherent limitations of current indicators, which analyze specific areas. The participants highlighted the importance of cross-referring data in order to take this accumulative cause and effect into account. This nonetheless remains a point which should be further examined.
- *Poverty and Liberty:* The utility emerges, from the different chapters approached, of looking at poverty in terms of the limitations it imposes on the ability to make choices, to build projects on one's own strengths or those of one's family, of giving a chosen orientation to one's existence and, in a general way, of exercising one's liberty.

Conclusions

The participants were consistently and above all guided by the realities of life as experienced by people living in poverty. This approach has not resulted in the creation of a list—more or less complete—of poverty indicators, even if concrete suggestions for such indicators were drawn up. The participants have exposed certain essential elements of poverty that are hardly, or not at all, being taken into account by current indicators. On this issue, they consider that the systematic and rigorous evaluation of measures to combat poverty as well as policies of prevention must find a recognized place in the process of investigating poverty indicators.

Their work thus constitutes a contribution to the putting into practice of Article 3 of the cooperative accord calling for continuity in the war on poverty in Belgium. This reflection is not yet closed.

Eco-Audit

Environmental Benefits Statement

The World Bank is committed to preserving Endangered Forests and natural resources. We print World Bank Working Papers and Country Studies on 100 percent postconsumer recycled paper, processed chlorine free. The World Bank has formally agreed to follow the recommended standards for paper usage set by Green Press Initiative—a nonprofit program supporting publishers in using fiber that is not sourced from Endangered Forests. For more information, visit www.greenpressinitiative.org.

In 2005, the printing of these books on recycled paper saved the following:

Trees*	Solid Waste	Water	Net Greenhouse Gases	Electricity
463	21,693	196,764	42,614	79,130
'40' in height and 6–8" in diameter	Pounds	Gallons	Pounds	KWH

green press INITIATIVE